The Guynd

The Guynd

A SCOTTISH JOURNAL

. . .

Belinda Rathbone

The Quantuck Lane Press

New York

FIRST PAPERBOUND EDITION, 2007

The text of this book is composed in Fournier
With the display set in Aquinas
Composition and book design by Barbara M. Bachman
Manufacturing by Maple-Vail Book Manufacturing Group
Map by David Lindroth

LIBRARY OF CONGRESS CATALOGING-IN-
PUBLICATION DATA

Rathbone, Belinda.

The Guynd : a Scottish journal / Belinda
Rathbone.— 1st ed.

p. cm.

ISBN 978-1-59372-025-4

1. Scotland—Social life and customs—
20th century. 2. Rathbone, Belinda—Homes and
haunts—Scotland. 3. Married people—Scotland.
4. Manors—Scotland. I. Title.

DA826.R38 2005

941.1085'9'092—dc22

2005003465

The Quantuck Lane Press, New York

Distributed by W.W. Norton & Company,
500 Fifth Avenue, New York, NY 10110

www.quantucklanepress.com

W.W. Norton & Company Ltd., Castle House,
75/76 Wells Street, London, WIT 3QT

2 3 4 5 6 7 8 9 0

For John and Elliot

Contents

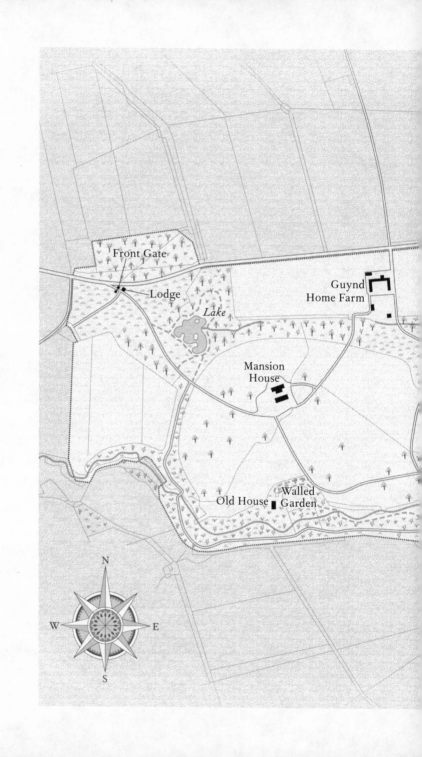

The Guynd

Temple

Elliot   Water

Part One

ONE

It's All Yours If You Want It

. . .

I KNEW WHEN I MARRIED THE MAN THAT I married the mansion. Though which would pose the greater challenge—my husband John, or his crumbling Georgian country house in northeast Scotland—there was no telling. There was no separating them, in mind or in fact. There was no dealing with one that did not involve the other, lurking somewhere in the background. For this was not just a house but the scene of my husband's childhood, of his father's childhood, of the labors and loves of his ancestors. It was the material proof of an ancient and once prominent Scottish family that is now close to extinction, and scarcely a day went by when we didn't feel the weight of its history upon us and the mandate to hang on.

Was anybody watching? Did the family ghosts smile with approval as we wheeled out the George III silver teapot and the Old Willow pattern teacups into the drawing room every afternoon at five o'clock? Did they sigh as we dropped into armchairs with sagging springs and faded upholstery in our stocking feet and blue jeans? Did they dismay at the sight of the peeling paint in the upper corners of our stately rooms, or the cobwebs clinging to the capitals, as we made a dive for the Safeway's shortbread in the crumb-ridden depths of a rusty biscuit tin?

We lived on the stage set of another era, or the kind of layering of several eras that happens when a family stays in one place for many generations—in this case a stylistic evolution from Regency through the postwar era. All the country house equipment was in place. The dining room cupboard stored regiments of cut glass bowls, decanters, wineglasses, demitasses, picnic boxes, saltcellars, fruit knives, dinner plates stamped with the family crest. Upstairs, the cedar-lined linen cupboard overflowed with a history of bed linen, damask table cloths, napkins, and embroidered hand towels. Downstairs the old wine cellar housed an archive of old prints and family portraits, miscellaneous frayed curtains, faded slipcovers, swords, broken lamps, empty preserve jars, and prewar pots and pans. The desk drawers were stuffed with diaries, bank statements, bills, schoolboys' letters home, assorted calling cards and dance cards dating back fifty years and more, and reams of pale blue stationery engraved on the upper right, "The Guynd, by Arbroath, Angus," and on the left, "Telephone, Carmyllie 250," boxed, waiting for the lady of the house, with her fountain pen.

The tool shed was a catalogue of mowers, rollers, rakes, trimmers and strimmers, loppers and scythes. What were once the laundry, the stable, the henhouse, and the coal store were now a jumble of cast-off furniture, farm vehicles in need of repair, and building scrap. The old vaulted kitchen was the living room of the East flat. The nursery was an artist's studio.

We had everything such a house required except for the nine servants who once took care of it. For some years Will Crighton, the retired gardener, came every morning to count the animals in the fields and every few days to mow the three and a half acres of lawn around the house. But I gave up trying to get anyone to help me clean. For I was the housekeeper and the chambermaid, the cook and the nanny. John was the gardener, the plumber, the launderer, and the odd-job man. Still, at the end of the day, as we sat fireside in the library amidst volumes such as *The Gardener's Chronicle, Burke's Peerage,* and Byron's leatherbound *Complete Poetical Works* and discussed what to do about a broken stone wall or an untidy tenant, he was the laird (the twenty-sixth), and I was the chatelaine.

WE MET IN VANCOUVER, at a cousin's wedding, in July 1990. The bride, my cousin Pippa, was equally John's cousin, as she was the daughter of my uncle and his aunt. Both of us had been especially urged to make the trek west for the wedding, I from New York and John from London, as the last of Pippa's assorted cousins to remain unmarried. We had met once before, as children; our families had converged in Italy back in 1954. But the age difference between us—thirteen and a half years—was then enough to make us almost unaware of each other. I was a toddler when he was a teenager.

At fifty-three John was still a bachelor. At thirty-nine so was I. Strategically, the family had arranged for us both to be put up for the weekend with the neighbors, an elderly Mr. and Mrs. Hamilton. When my taxi pulled in from the airport at dusk, a lanky dark-haired figure lurched out of the house to help me with my bags.

This must be John.

Inside, over a drink with our hosts, I watched his long, lean figure unfold awkwardly into a chair, like a youth still searching for the right fit, as we attempted to ground ourselves in relation to our Canadian cousins and catch up on the last thirty-some years.

His talk was witty, ironic, and charged with nervous energy. As he darted nimbly from one subject to the next, he revealed an upper-class British background, but without the superficial polish. If he was the product of a system at all he was an errant one. He used words like salubrious with ease and relish, but he also peppered his speech with colloquial British expressions such as naff and bloke that gave it a tougher edge. Though his accent was English his features were somehow of a rarer breed or more ancient genesis. His long face, though lined, showed the youthful softness of a moist climate. His high, bony cheeks were shot through with the ruddy rose that comes from the chill of stone buildings in winter, and his gray-blue eyes beamed steadily out of their sheltered hollows. When he laughed you could see the gold in his back teeth.

We sat together at the Catholic wedding service the next day, whispering expressions of impatience with the Latin. During the reception at the Capilano Golf Club John hovered, bringing me canapés and topping up my champagne. After the wedding some of us went out for supper at a noisy pub in downtown Vancouver, where we ate hamburgers and shouted and laughed over the din of the loud music. John pulled me onto the dance floor and we rocked and rolled, losing track of our party in the reeling crowd.

On Monday we took off for Denman Island to stay with Pippa's older sister Anne on her organic apple farm. Our knees knocked together in the crowded backseat of Anne's station wagon. We bundled up against the wind and strolled the rolling deck of the ferryboat. The next morning John and I were promptly dispatched on an outing with bicycles and directed toward the ferry to nearby Hornby Island. John, leading the way, wagged his tail at me like a happy dog and cast the occasional backward glance as I strove to keep up. We found a sandy beach, went swimming in the cool blue bay, shared sandwiches, and swapped travel stories.

"I don't like being a tourist," I told him. "Nowadays I tend go where I'm invited, either on business or as a guest in somebody's house. It's the only way to really get into the heart of a place."

"I just like exploring, without a fixed program," John rejoined—much as we were doing that day, cycling down unknown roads without a map, without a guide. We had both spent time in Spain on business. We discussed the

Spanish character, and that famous cliché, mañana. Did their use of the word really mean that they could put something off indefinitely, I queried, or, on the contrary, that it was urgent? John thought it meant they could put it off. In my experience it meant that it was urgent. Perhaps our sense of the Spanish character simply served as a mirror of ourselves. John's instinct to put things off and my sense of urgency meant that in this case we almost, but not quite, missed the last ferry back to Denman.

That evening after supper, sitting around the picnic table on the porch of Anne's self-built island farmhouse, Anne asked John about "the Guynd," his family home in Scotland, which she remembered visiting as a child.

The Guynd, I learned, was an agricultural estate that John's family had owned for the past four hundred years. "Guynd" in Gaelic means "a high, marshy place." The Guynd rhymes with "the wind," and as it blew into our conversation the residual gaiety of the wedding weekend was swept away like a summer shower on a picnic. No longer the convivial traveler, John's expression darkened; a flood of concerns and irritations surrounded and enveloped him. He had resumed the role he'd left behind in Scotland, that of the reluctant incumbent to a sadly run-down estate.

Since his mother's death three years earlier the mansion house had stood empty, except for a single tenant, a young artist from Glasgow, in a basement flat. John's father had been dead some twenty years. John's younger brother, Angus, had left his wife and three children and fled to Canada back in the 1970s. John himself had been residing at a safe distance, in London, for the past several years. Trained as a mechanical engineer, he had been caught up in the ferment of the 1960s, gave up a career in the oil business, and never looked back. From then on, between roaming South America with a girlfriend, boat building in Majorca for a rich American, and flat renovating all over London, he discovered sex, marijuana, garlic, and William H. Whyte's *The Organization Man* and decided he was a new man. Meanwhile he continued to make regular forays to Scotland, knowing that the house would someday be his, as the elder son, to carry on. For no matter what experience he had acquired elsewhere, and what attractions they held, his identity was still shaped mainly by that role and that place.

"When are you going to move back?" asked Anne.

"I get up there quite a lot," John answered defensively. "Anyway, Stephen's in the West flat. He's always there." The question bothered him, I could tell. It was clear that his inheritance was a mixed blessing, that as much as he was devoted to the memory—or myth—of its glorious past, the reality of its present condition was discouraging at best. The appearance of the light traveler with his backpack, the breezy cyclist who just liked to explore, concealed an unusually heavy load of baggage that weighed him down wherever he went. Although we shared first cousins, and my mother was born as English as his was, we were of very different cultures.

From an early age I had traveled widely in Europe with my family, and we never failed to schedule a stay in

England. I have fond childhood memories of visiting my cousin Judith in her long, low-ceilinged cottage in the Kent countryside, of climbing the cherry trees and walking the fields with her dogs. I remember staying at the Norfolk Hotel in South Kensington, riding the double-decker bus to Covent Garden, and feeding the ducks in Hyde Park. In school, for some reason, my eyes watered and my voice choked when we sang "Jerusalem." But what did building Jerusalem in England's green and pleasant land have to do with me? Now I knew, as I listened to John, that I had only skimmed the surface. He had a depth, a kind of world-weariness that is the privilege of Europeans—especially Europeans with baggage—that I could hardly touch.

The scene he described in Scotland was like something out of *Country Life*. I recalled the magazine arriving for my mother once a month in a brown, tightly rolled overseas bundle, and I would peruse the front pages with its aerial views of vast manorial estates hidden deep in the English countryside, or thatched roof cottages that might have been the setting of a Thomas Hardy novel. To John the scene was not that of a book or a magazine; it was real, it was today, the characters were living, and he was one of them.

Anne had assigned me to a bedroom upstairs, and John to a mattress on the living room floor. But that night I crept downstairs. My plane was leaving *mañana*, in a matter of hours we would be separated by thousands of miles, and there was no time to worry about propriety. Besides, as I slid under the covers beside John, I could tell he was expecting me.

The next afternoon John saw me off from the little island airfield, promising to write and to call, and to plan our next meeting. But where? John was eager to come to New York but I was hesitant to see him there just yet. He seemed to be a man trying to escape his past, and I was not sure I was prepared to play host to his flight. Better, I thought, to see him first on his own turf, to know what he was running from. We agreed to meet at the Edinburgh Festival in late August. That way, if our precipitous, long-distance romance proved a fizzle, we could always lose ourselves in the darkness of the theater.

"BRING PLENTY OF WARM CLOTHES," warned my mother, "it's not like summer there."

In August? My mother had a tendency to exaggerate, especially about the cold. I traveled in a thin cotton dress and regretted it the minute I stepped outside the terminal building at the Edinburgh airport. A brisk wind whipped at my skirts as I buttoned up my cardigan and searched for a sign of John. There he was, the native, in a heavy shirt and pullover, corduroys and sandals with socks. (Sandals with socks!) Everything that had seemed exotic or eccentric about John in Vancouver was about to seem perfectly normal. He was a cut of the old cloth.

In Edinburgh at festival time the one-act plays, comedy revues, and concerts of the "fringe" played in every available public space, and clowns and mimes performed their antics on the hilly, cobbled streets of the Old Town. Walking the streets with names like Cowgate and Grass-

market, overlooked by the stony fortress of Edinburgh
Castle at one end of the town and the bare hillside of the
Crags at the other, John was in his element, and I was
entranced. We laughed through parodies of Shakespeare's
tragedies, dozed through a theatrical rendition of *Finne-
gans Wake,* and danced Scottish reels in an old town hall.
John shouted instructions and madly waved his arms at me
as I was whirled from one partner to the next in the rollicking "Strip the Willow." When we came out sweating it
was well past midnight but the streets were still hot with
activity. Finally we returned to our little blue room at Mrs.
Reekie's B and B and made love in one of the twin beds
before collapsing in utter exhaustion.

Between the distractions of the festival, as we relaxed
over tea or a beer, conversation inevitably turned again
and again to the Guynd. John rambled. His answers to my
questions were not always easy to follow. He had a way of
hurrying through some subjects, then taking long circuitous routes around the point of another, as if the idea
was to keep his listener in the dark. I had a feeling that the
place was on his mind all the time, even when he was
asleep. Sometimes, awake, lost in thought, his face would
twitch and contort, engaged in some angry exchange with
one of his many demons. He was not in the habit of shar-
ing his thoughts as much as battling them out alone. The
only thing that seemed clear, from where we now sat just
fifty-odd miles south of the Guynd in an Edinburgh café,
was that I could not carry on the conversation much fur-

ther without meeting his albatross face to face. All right, he eventually, reluctantly, agreed, we could dash up to the Guynd for a night or two, maybe visit friends in Fife or Perthshire on the way to or from, to take the edge off the point of our main destination.

In his mother's dusty gold VW Scirocco we left Edinburgh, crossed the Firth of Forth into Fife, and drove through a hilly, pastoral landscape for another thirty miles or so. Crossing the Tay Bridge we entered the big, gray town of Dundee and the county of Angus. We stopped for groceries at a supermarket at the far end of town, agreeing on chicken for dinner, eggs for breakfast. From there onward the route was along narrow, winding country roads. John grew silent. As he shifted gears I could tell he knew every bend. Finally he slowed at a junction where a small weather-beaten wooden sign pointing to the right read, "Guynd—½ mile." His profile tightened as we approached a low, ivy-covered wall and the stone lodge at the head of the front drive.

Passing through the iron gates, John unstrapped his seat belt as if to relieve some of his tension at the prospect of coming home. He suddenly turned hawklike in his attention to a rut in the road here, an untidy edge of lawn there. He muttered to himself things that were too obscure for me to understand. He was talking to himself anyway. We had left the world of the present and had entered the long tunnel of his past.

To my American eyes the landscape appeared lush and

orderly, mature rather than overgrown. As we drove the half mile from the main road to the house, an acre of lawn suddenly opened up on the left, edged with abundant rhododendrons, followed by shadowy woods of towering beech trees. Then the landscape opened wide with a pasture on the right, huge oaks and sycamores dotting it here and there, shading the grazing cattle and, on the left, a freshly plowed field. Straight ahead in the distance on a slight rise, surrounded with tall trees and shrubs, I could see the house.

Late Georgian, its neoclassical lines somewhat weather-worn at the edges, the house is of a style that strikes the average American as something more to do with a bank or a post office than a family home. It reminded me of a picture I had grown up with that hung in our dining room of a Regency house designed by my great-great-great grandfather in England, which had always puzzled me as a child. They called this a house? Now here it was, as if the watercolor had come alive. That this style could have been considered, in its heyday, "informal," that its strict symmetry was designed to relate to a romantic landscape, takes some time and study on the American's part to fully understand. For the time being it was enough to take in its sheer bulk of stone. It was enough to wonder, as we approached the front portico, what a house like this one was doing with a pair of ordinary storm doors painted institutional green, inset with wired glass windows.

John fumbled with a collection of keys on a string and opened the heavy double doors, then the big front door. We entered a vast front hall. It smelled damp, the damp of stone walls and old carpets and I didn't know what else. Its far corners were rounded by fourteen-foot classical columns and matching pilasters, all of them painted black. The walls had faded from whatever they once were to a nondescript beige. An old Turkish carpet of pale green and orange covered the stone floor. A single bare lightbulb hung from the ceiling. A mass of tools and bric-a-brac littered a table in one of the far corners. A wicker dog basket, padded with a shredded blanket, presided over another. A large armchair shouldered the overflow from the cloakroom. There were two alcoves containing bronze boy figures of unknown origin on pedestals, one of them adorned with a paper party hat, and two grandfather clocks, one to the right, the other straight ahead under the stairs, neither ticking.

Beyond the pillars the stone staircase was piled with things on their way somewhere, up or down. A begonia plant with large pointed waxy leaves, which at first glance I thought was plastic, had been trained to wind its way up the banister. Looking up, I discovered the source of light the begonia was heading for—a huge round glass cupola with wrought-iron filigree, edged with the grime of condensation.

Instantly John abandoned the role of host that he had played with such flair in Edinburgh. I looked on in some confusion as he followed his distracted thoughts from one source of anxiety to another, dodging about and disappearing into dark cluttered passages and behind doors, then appearing again out of another, clutching the odd tool, suddenly remembering that I was there, not quite sure what to do about it. "Are you all right? Do you need anything?"

I couldn't think what I needed. "No, no I'm fine." Anyway, I was apparently being left on my own to explore.

Opening a pair of large veneered double doors off the front hall, I discovered the dining room. More Ionic columns, this time white, formed a screen at the far end of the room. The windows were tall and generous and the walls were faded Wedgwood blue. A baroque painting of the Madonna and Child, punctured and patched with what appeared to be a wad of tar, occupied the wall between the columns. Ancestor to my left—a pleasant-faced late Georgian gentleman with a bemused smile. Ancestor to my right—a rather more determined-looking Victorian. On the dining room table dust had gathered around the place mats, left from a dinner party some months ago. More chairs than I could count. A small table on the side draped in cloth as thick as a blanket held a white metal plate warmer, such as you might see in a rooming house. A variety of vintage electric space heaters stationed in the far corners assured me that this was a cold room in winter, perhaps even in spring. The floor was covered, inexplicably, with stained puddle-brown linoleum.

On the other side of the front hall, directly opposite the dining room, a matching pair of doors opened into the library. Bookshelves built into deep architraves, stocked with leather-bound volumes and edged with a bedraggled leather dust fringe, gave off the faint glint of faded gold leaf. A clutter of souvenirs and children's toys littered the shelves in front of the books. Color picture postcards curled with damp lined the white marble mantel piece. Half empty tonic and gin bottles sprouted from the drinks tray behind an enormous armchair covered in brown stretch fabric. But how to get across this room, past the barricade of oversize armchairs, huge standard lamps with their cockeyed shades, a giant television, an old hi-fi system built into a table, three-and-a-half-foot speakers covered with pink psychedelic fabric, and through the curtained archway straight ahead?

Picking my way across the room I drew the curtain and passed through the arch into a spacious drawing room, bright even with the shades drawn. Three windows at the far end, facing southwest, flanked the bowed end of the house. Dodging a collection of dead flies on the windowsill, I gave the shades a tug and revealed with a snap a living triptych of fields and trees. Another large window on the left framed an ancient copper beech and shed a shaft of light on the keyboard of the grand piano. It was a hall of mirrors and glass: gold-leafed mirror brackets over marquetry game tables in the niches of either side of the fireplace, a huge mirror over the mantel, and overhead a Bohemian glass chandelier, dripping with prisms. A hard-edged art deco drawing room suite, covered in wrinkled pink damask slipcovers, dominated the middle of the room. This was clearly the lady's end of the house, her showpiece. I imagined John's mother serving tea.

In spite of its glorious light, its air of gentility, and its fine antiques, the drawing room depressed me as much as any other. Perhaps even more so, because of the effort implied in making it cheerful and elegant and, above all, correct. There was nowhere in the house where I felt I could sit down and relax without feeling the massiveness of the gloom that surrounded me.

As I climbed the stairs my heart sank even lower. The landing was heaped high with old curtains and cushions, a glass-fronted bookcase stood half empty, books all askew, as if it had been hastily scoured and relieved of its choicest treasures. Wherever I looked I felt the stillness of John's mother's death three years before, and the disarray following the task of sorting her belongings. Various relatives had made their passes through, taken what they wanted, and vanished. What they left behind was drained of life and tainted with rejection.

I had always thought of myself, having grown up in New England, as someone well prepared to confront the baggage and the bumps of an old family place. I had known enough old Boston families, old money, deeply imbued with the ethic of inconspicuous consumption, to appreciate the beauty of an unrenovated country kitchen, the charm of faded upholstery, and the clutter of dusty heirlooms. But this was not the warm, drab grandeur of an old summer house in Manchester-by-the-Sea. This was not the cherished family retreat in the White Mountains of New Hampshire or the lakeside log cabin camp in the Adirondacks. Love must once have been felt for this place, but it was not the kind that passes like a gift from one generation to the next in the name of summertime pleasures and memories. This was the centerpiece of a system gone to seed, deeply suggestive of the forbidden desire to give up and get out. Some hidden force kept them there, but it wasn't exactly love.

I felt a strong urge to start moving things around, but I didn't know where to begin. I decided to take a walk.

I found John around the back of the house, immersed in a sea of tools and spare parts in a vast skylit garage. He was working on the brake system of his mother's Scirocco. Now that we were here I wondered if I would ever be able to tear him away, as he was already in the grip of so many problems. A young man with wavy brown hair was trying to get John's attention. Turning to me he introduced himself as Stephen, the artist who lived in the basement flat at the West end of the house, the one who was always there. And that was Foxy, the yellow Labrador Stephen had been looking after while John was away. It was clear that no one could be bade to accompany me on anything so unnecessary as a walk, not even the dog.

"She won't go with you," said John, "doesn't know you well enough." But he assured me that I couldn't get lost if I simply followed "the circuit."

On my own I followed the invitation of a road just in front of the house, which led between two fields. My heart lifted at the sight of a gigantic sycamore before me, its massive trunk holding a perfectly shaped crown of deep green leaves. There was a fair breeze. The sky was big and near and clouds moved rapidly across the blue; the sun winked in and out, angling across a field of wheat. A pheasant squawked and fluttered out of the tall grass in front of me. Handsome old specimen trees dotted here and there in the fields made the scene look not so much like a farm as resembling a pleasure park. Now rounding a corner and looking back across a field of grazing beasts I caught sight of the house in the distance, perhaps a quarter mile from where I stood. I suddenly imagined myself a character in a Jane Austen novel. There was nothing in my view that declared the arrival of the twentieth century. I wouldn't have been surprised to see a horse and buggy wheeling by. For the most essential thing—the house and its command of the landscape—had as much authority as it would have had two hundred years ago.

I FOUND JOHN in the kitchen, a narrow room on the north side of the house with strangely high ceilings. It was chilly. There was no need to refrigerate the chicken we had bought for supper, which sat next to the sink in its plastic wrapping. The wooden counter around the sink looked damp and had a lip along its edge, like a ship's galley, as if to keep things from sliding off in case of a storm. The narrow workspace was cluttered with a collection of toasters and weighing scales and big crockery jars stuffed with wooden implements. An overworked roll of flypaper hung in a twirl from a fluorescent light fixture. A long terry-cloth hand towel hung from a wooden roller in a loop and looked overdue for a thorough laundering.

"Used to be the butler's pantry," said John. "The

original kitchen was downstairs on the basement level, just below us. Now it's the main room of the East flat."

"Isn't it awfully far from the dining room?" I asked naively.

"That was the whole point. You weren't supposed to smell cooking until it was on a plate in front of you. It was a bit of a trek for the maids, though, with their platters of hot food, scurrying up and down the stone stairs. Though of course there was also the dumbwaiter." He opened a sliding, square door to a wobbly shelf at counter level, where a large aluminum pot was parked. "I sometimes keep a head of lettuce in there. Better than the fridge, really. Anyway, why not save a watt?"

"Why not," I agreed, somewhat mystified.

"How about a drink?"

I couldn't think of anything I needed more. Ice cubes could be wrested from a frost-ridden, doorless freezer compartment in a bar-sized fridge.

"I never use ice," said John, which was plain to see. "Unnecessary in this climate."

We would not be eating dinner in the dining room that night, I was relieved to hear. It was too cold, and too big for the two of us. Instead, as John used to do with his mother, we wheeled our trolley of food out of the kitchen and into the library. John unfolded a little Pembroke table in front of the sofa, drew up a chair on the other side, and lit a fire.

In the dim light of two undersized table lamps and the warm sparkle of the fire, I could forget for a moment the miserable clutter and dowdiness of this once proud room.

We had, for the evening, claimed for ourselves a little corner of it and brought it to life. John laid our table for two with sturdy place mats, the family silverware, chipped kitchen plates, saltcellar and pepper grinder, seersucker napkins. With a pair of grape scissors he snipped fresh parsley over our boiled potatoes.

"Duke of York, these are, earlies."

Whatever that meant.

"First crop of the season," added John, relishing the prospect. He brightened the fire with a few gentle blows of the bellows, then took a little hearth broom and swept the ashes away from the lip of the Franklin stove and into a shovel. The inscrutable Foxy stretched herself elegantly across the fire stool and closed her eyes.

There was so much to learn.

"What are all these books about?" I began. "Have you read any of them?"

"Oh sure. Well, some," he answered. "They're about all sorts of things—poetry over in that corner, English history down there, estate management, gardening, architecture, that sort of thing, over here. A lot of them were bought by subscription." He stabbed a spud with his fork. "Sometimes you find that the pages haven't even been cut."

"That's an elaborate cornice," I said, gazing upward. "Is there some symbolism there? I see a crown."

"That was one of my in-laws, Elizabeth Grant. She was supposed to have descended from three kings, thus the three crowns. They just made that stuff by the yard, from a mold."

"The cornice was made by the yard?"

John enjoyed exposing the hard practical reality behind things that were held as mysterious or sacred. At the same time his attention to detail, his care for breakable objects and delicate surfaces, and his respect for old things and genteel rituals reminded me of my father. An art connoisseur, museum director, and auction house adviser, my father had brought me up to respect antiques and objects of beauty. John's sense of how things worked, of the logic and economics behind their construction, gave the quality of his care a different emphasis that was new to me. For my father, appearance and presentation were inextricable from the object itself. Never far from the front of his mind was the art of seducing his public with his careful display, of creating a dialogue between the object and its surroundings. All of this went along naturally with his courtly manners and his well-tailored clothes. While my father knew how to dress the outside, John understood how to fix the inside. If my father was a master of form, John was a master of function. John approached things from underneath, deeply involved in their mechanisms. He was too accustomed to the wealth of his possessions, too engaged with the process of their repair and maintenance to notice the superficial disarray he might be causing on the surface.

Or was it just that John—even at fifty-three—was not yet ready to play the host to his heritage? Pride of place seemed to be hidden under several layers of humility. About its grandeur, which he was not sure he could live up to, on the one hand. About its present state of disorder, which he was not sure he could live down, on the other. Which was the greater burden to bear?

"How long has your family owned the Guynd?" I asked him.

"Nearly four hundred years. They moved over from a castle called Kelly, just a couple miles from here. The original Guynd house is over there," he said, gesturing out the window. "This one is of course relatively modern, designed in 1799."

"It all depends on your perspective, I guess."

I wasn't sure he heard me. "How does the farm work? Do you have tenants in all these fields?" I asked.

"A fellow called Webster up the road has a long-term lease on the arable, you know, barley, wheat—cereal crops. Then the grass is auctioned off by the season for the beef."

"The grass?"

"Grass, as in pasture. Grazing. Don't you call it grass in America?"

"No, I don't think we do. And we don't call it *the beef*, either."

"Well, the beasts then."

Though these farm tenants provided an income, John explained, it was no longer enough to sustain a large house, the farm buildings, and the grounds, as it used to be in the old days. As history neared the present we approached John's nerve center. His comments became intense and emotional, his characters more clearly defined in black and white. There was his unhappy mother, who tried so hard, and his stern, distant father. There were the greedy accountants and the useless estate managers who were out for themselves, and there was the galloping overdraft. The Guynd was not yet John's, though he was its sole beneficiary. It was still in the hands of trustees his father had appointed many years ago. There seemed to be a few legalities of the so-called trust deed to unravel before the estate could be turned over to him. Something about his brother Angus's share of the inheritance. Something else about a farmer with a long-term lease, which under the new law was to have expired three years ago but who refused to leave. Something about a timber merchant who had harvested three acres of woods but hadn't reinstated the roads he'd messed up in the process. I couldn't follow it all. I had left *Mansfield Park* and entered *Bleak House*.

We took the master bedroom at the East end of the house, which had been badly painted aqua blue. A gloomy gray print of a river scene hung over the fireplace, which was blocked by a large suitcase. Twin beds had been shoved together and a double mattress slung over the top of them to create the only double bed in the house. We went to sleep between a flannel sheet and a winter-weight duvet, with the heavy curtains pulled tight against the early summer dawn.

How strange this all was to me, fresh from New York, where what matters is not where you come from but what you are doing there, not what happened years ago but what is happening now. I had been steeped in the art world, living in a distillation of many cultures, sampling its riches, its variety, its ethnic pockets, floating above it all in a society of commentary and intellect. New York, I had been led to believe, was the center of the world. The very air you breathed would bring you up to date with the latest in everything. But about what? And who cared? It made no difference to anything here in Scotland. The oblivion I felt was pleasantly disconcerting. The materiality of those ancient trees put everything else in its proper perspective. The sense of primal attachment to the land— the land of one's forefathers—was hard to refute. With his ancient ties to this storybook scene, John offered an adventure I didn't even know I was looking for. Still, I wondered, how could I, in my American way, help him to realize a viable future for a crippled estate and the dwindling remains of a family, now among the *ancienne pauvre* that cling steadfastly to the mast of their aristocratic ship as it goes down?

When we drove to London a week later to catch my plane at Heathrow, my head spun with these questions, while John, his sharp eyes on the road, was quiet and tense. Saying good-bye, amidst the hasty confusion of checking bags, rummaging for my passport and ticket, and the bustle of other anxious travelers, John threw up his hands in one final gesture and cried, "It's all yours if you want it!"

TWO

Heir and Spare

. . .

"YOU'LL NEVER GET ANY PLEASURE FROM THIS PLACE," John's father had told him repeatedly over the years. And by most accounts other than his own, he made every effort, or lack of effort, possible to ensure that his prediction would prove accurate, and that his eldest son—his principal heir—would fail at the role fate had dealt him.

The ancient system of primogeniture, which decrees that the eldest son is heir to the entire family estate, is still going strong in Scotland. From birth he is groomed, pressed, and molded by family and society into his role as landowner—in Scotland, the *laird*. Primogeniture is based on a feudal system that has changed remarkably little since the Middle Ages. While in England the march of progress and the greater population have blurred the rigid lines of the class system in recent times, Scotland still offers a clear window on the past. Its unspoiled view of the pastoral countryside of the Lowlands, and of the vast shooting estates of the Highlands, owe much to the persistence of primogeniture. Eighty-eight percent of Scotland is privately owned, and if you buy one of those clan maps they make for the Scottish tourist trade, you will find that it is still largely owned by the families who drew the lines centuries ago.

The landed classes. Since knowing John I have come to better understand the meaning of this term. In Scotland it means not only that these people have land but, once landed, that they intend to stay. Forever. It is almost as much of a personal failure for a Scottish male heir to leave the ancestral home behind him (read, lack of commitment) as it is for the American to stay (read, lack of enterprise). It is no accident that in colloquial Scots, when they ask someone where they live, they ask them where do they "stay." In Scotland it is not so much that one owns a country house as much as it is the other way around. In America, though we could all trace our family history through various houses and buildings, few among us know where they are, or if indeed they are still standing. And we don't really care. After all, we Americans are largely the descendants of second sons who expected to strike out on their own.

I was raised with a relatively strong sense of my own family history. On my father's side the Dutch merchant class of New York City and upstate crossed with Puritan New Englanders. When I was a child my grandmother still lived in the Greek Revival house that her grandfather had built in 1830 on the main street of Greene, New York. Everything in that house, from the pair of stuffed pheasants on the dining room sideboard to the old toys in the attic, was woven into a warm, fragile tapestry of my father's American childhood. On my mother's side, worldly and artistic Europeans with intermarriages of French, Italian, and English connected in her parents' marriage with a long line of Quaker Philadelphians. At home in Cambridge, Massachusetts, I grew up with antiquities collected by my great-aunt when she lived in Egypt, Victorian furniture from the house of my Philadelphia great-great-grandparents, Irish glassware, and French china. There were family portraits in oil, silhouette, and daguerreotype. These family treasures came together in our own house from so many different sources, now mixed with my father's collections of modern European art, English Delftware, and pre-Columbian pottery, that the pieces of my family history took years for me to unravel. In spite of these tangible artifacts there were so many sources, names, places, and stories to remember about them. So few cousins, so far away. There was no tying them in with a single family house or even a single family name.

It was the critical difference between my background and John's. John could reach into his family history effortlessly, with hardly a leap of the imagination, for the stage was still set in his native Scotland. On the shelves of the library he could handle the very books his ancestors had consulted. He was sitting in their chairs, looking into their mirrors, literally walking in their footsteps, shaded by the trees they had planted, sheltered by the house they had built, and carrying on the same name. This was continuity to be envied. Yet it comes with a price.

In Scotland a man of John's class is himself less important than his name, his ancestral home, and his estate. He is merely a link in the long family line stretching before and after him, and his duty is clear: to keep it up. Americans may be fascinated by the British royal family and the role of the queen as figurehead. But this isn't just pageantry, or the stuff of gossip columns. The royal family sits at the pinnacle of the class system that is still very much in place and in power, especially outside of London, as it descends down the scale to the dukes, marquises, earls, viscounts, barons, and country squires. Rural gentry like those of John's family, though untitled, have stood their ground for so long that they are equally depended upon to remain in place as part of the stonework of society's foundations. All are part of the general effort to keep things just the way they have always been, and to a remarkable degree still are. While in school I was raised on stories of the pilgrims, the early homesteaders, the gold rush, and the life ethic conveyed by Emerson's "Self-Reliance," of Thoreau's "castles in the air," and Whitman's "Song of Myself"; John was made to memorize a succession of kings and queens. Thus I grew up with one myth of the possible—of wide-open spaces and eternal movement—and John grew up with another, that of the security of a closed gate at the end of the drive.

THE SUMMER BEFORE we were married I spent two months at the Guynd, from late June to late August. Was it true, I needed to know, what John's father had said— that he would never get any pleasure from this place— when it showed all the potential for being a paradise? In what way was he meant to defy his father's fatalistic words?

Since my first visit to the Guynd, our courtship had carried on in New York and in London, where John still had a flat. We had also traveled together, getting to know each other's friends and family, daily life and work. No American beau of mine had ever been so open, so curious, and so delighted by the people and places I had to show him. He arrived in New York with all the exuberance of a schoolboy let out to play or a sailor home from the sea. In my apartment, the top floor of a brownstone on East Ninety-second Street, he quickly made himself at home, unpacking his gray duffel (hiking boots, a few shirts, a bow tie or two just in case of an occasion, and a quantity of loose tea, not quite trusting that the right thing could be found in New York City), puttering in the kitchen (don't you have a wok? where do you put the compost?), and sinking into the sofa with the *Financial Times* (delighted to find he could buy it out of a box on the corner of Fifth Avenue).

He read anything I put in his hands, ate anything I put on the table (his plate as conscientiously scraped as if a dog had licked it), looked with unequivocal interest at anything and everything in any museum or gallery I took him to in New York, not to mention everything on the way there. It was exhausting. But his dogged attention to detail slowed the rush of the city, and his observant foreign eye and the swift backhand stroke of his wit lightened my step on the pavement. His engineer's logic combined with a bracing cynicism and a nose for the corrupt. All sorts of badly made things, for instance, were "good for business!" he'd say triumphantly. He'd caught the devil at his game.

His intimate understanding of materials brought another way of appreciating almost everything, including works of art. "Wood," he might offer, admiring a work of modern sculpture, "is difficult to work with, in that it's delicate and unpredictable, whereas metal is isotropic. It does what you tell it to." Isotropic. A brick wall curved in a continuous wave pattern, which I assumed was purely an aesthetic choice on the part of its maker, was very practical, according to John. "A sinuous wall is self-buttressing, and therefore doesn't need to be as thick as a straight wall." The meaning of objects took on a whole new dimension. They had lives—even minds—of their own. A string, John told me in all seriousness, has a memory.

My friends regarded John as something of an exotic, unable to measure his worthiness on the usual scale. He had a wiry energy; there was something embattled and vulnerable about him, but also a toughness born to a tough breed. He seemed to be on intimate terms with the earth, the way a Scot—not an Englishman—would be. The reputation of his rather large house in the country awarded him a mysterious status. He was an old world radical, an aristocratic country rustic. He used arcane expressions such as "the nether regions" and "in days of yore" as if he really meant them. He possessed a depth of practical know-how and a living sense of history they couldn't quite touch. With my mother he was completely at home; he knew she appreciated that depth, that sense, without having to say so, like a silent pact among the European-born. At times I felt they understood each other better than I understood either of them. They shared the tough-mindedness of survivors, an ethic of simplicity and economy, a conscientious reading of newspapers, and a passion for plain, dark chocolate.

Visiting me in America, John said, was like a dream. How funny. It was the Guynd that was like a dream to me. He departed after a month with a reluctant flurry of last-minute packing to head back to the loneliness of his responsibilities.

Alone again in New York I listened to the strains of Elgar's *Enigma Variations* and the soundtrack of *A Room with a View,* stared at the ceiling, and wondered what was happening to me like some modern-day Henry James character, the innocent American about to be plunged into the murky depths of European aristocracy.

The responsibilities of the Guynd seemed awesome to me and yet, for some reason, I had been chosen. What was the point of romance anyway, I had always thought, if it wasn't to take you somewhere you never expected to go, to make you intimate with a place or a culture in a way no other route could take you, to start life all over again from scratch, as a stranger in a strange land. Or, perhaps, in this case, to mend a broken connection, to complete the cycle back to my mother's British upbringing. It was as if I were answering to some cosmic force. The beauty and the poignancy of the Guynd haunted me; it seemed to have called upon me to awaken it, a dollhouse gathering dust in the attic. And John's ardent pursuit showed no signs of letting up, even over the course of many weeks and an ocean apart. With no warning his excited voice from a phone box in London (breathless, out cycling in the rain, just had to call) would jar the streamlined images I had formed of my safe future as a New Yorker.

We became engaged on the night train from Paris to Zurich. This was thanks to my English cousin Cecilia, who lived outside of Paris and who was like an older sister to me. She had met us for dinner on our last evening there and presented me with a cameo brooch from among her family treasures "as an engagement present." Though marriage was a prospect we had both been studying seriously in our separate minds, we had not said anything to each other about getting engaged. After dinner in a crowded bistro Cecilia hurried us into a taxi to catch our train, beaming with goodwill and happiness for us, and we chuckled along with her excitement. We had booked ourselves into the most unromantic of sleeping arrangements possible, the third-class *couchette*. While travelers with backpacks mumbling other languages staggered through the door and wrestled themselves into their narrow cots below us and the train lurched through the night, we held hands across the two top berths, laughed, and agreed that Cecilia's gift had more or less confirmed what we already knew.

STILL, THE BIG TEST was ahead of us that summer. Was John really able to share his past with another, and was I equipped to take it on?

At the time I was at work on a biography of the American photographer Walker Evans. Much of the research was behind me, at least enough to spend two months writing without resorting to my original sources. I had packed some seventy pounds of notes, as it weighed in at Kennedy airport, and John had invited me to take over his mother's sewing room as my study.

This was the brightest and prettiest room upstairs, straight across the landing. Designed as an upstairs sitting room, it was more or less square with the intriguing feature of a rounded interior wall. A fireplace anchored the rounded wall on one side, and to the right of it, under a gilt-edged mirror hung high, was a lady's desk. Its drawers were crammed with bundled letters, unwritten postcards, rubber bands, old photographs, and dozens of used *Vogue* sewing patterns from the 1960s. The desktop, folded down, was just big enough for my laptop computer. A 1930s radio provided a suitable stand for my printer. There was an outlet nearby, though of course not the right fit for my American equipment. John would fix that.

Through two generous windows I looked out over the tenants' grazing Angus cattle in the field in front of the house, the dark woods beyond, and, still farther, five miles as the crow flies, the straight horizontal line of the North Sea, reflecting a silvery blue or iron gray sky and sometimes disappearing completely in the fog.

Here, thousands of miles from the America of Walker Evans, I would use the steady tranquillity of this room to delve into his life and his art. His photographs of small-town storefronts, billboards and circus posters, rows of Victorian gingerbread houses, or Model T Fords parked along a rainy street seemed all the more quaintly American at this remove, and all the more touching. Evans had wanted, he said, to capture what something would someday look like as the past. He understood how profoundly the simplest thing—and often the neglected or rejected object—defined its moment. How did he acquire this visionary instinct for the telling detail? This fondness for the would-be forgotten? What aspects of his childhood had conspired to develop this genius? Somewhere in my notes was the stuff of the answer. I set to work.

Yet as every writer knows there is nothing more tempting than manual labor to arouse one from one's chair and give up the torturous task of writing. In a house like this one, even the simple movement of going downstairs to the kitchen to make another cup of coffee had the disadvantage of reminding me of the fifteen jobs vying equally for my attention.

On my way back upstairs I might pick up a rag and a

tin of wax to polish the wooden banister, enjoying the gleam of walnut veneer sliding under my flannel, emerging like a photograph in the developing bath. By cleaning and polishing I would become intimate with the house; I would arouse its dormant sparkle to waken and talk back to me. The ironwork supporting the banister needed dusting—no, rubbing, with a damp cloth—to appreciate that it was actually jet black, not gray. Back at the top of the stairs I would contemplate how to cope with the pile of old curtains and cushions that seemed for no reason to be heaped on top of a chaise longue, where clearly no one had ever been expected to lounge. Defeated by this problem for the moment, back at my keyboard, I set my mind to work again over a few precious clues to Evans's childhood. Foxy curled up on the floor behind me, waiting for the beep of my computer shutting down, knowing that then it would be time for a walk.

As much as the urge to clean had never felt more powerful, so also was I increasingly curious about John's family history, a family that was about to be mine. While I was learning the story from John, bit by bit, there were many gaps in his information. I also knew, as the biographer knows, how differently the story might be told by other voices in other times. Later, after work, after a walk, I was determined to look more closely at a diary I had discovered in the library downstairs. Wedged between Johnson's *Dictionary of the English Language* and a stack of atlases, its black leather cover bulged with promising content, buckled tight with two thin leather straps.

It was John's grandfather's, Colonel Thomas Ouch-terlony.

The name Ouchterlony, pronounced Och-ter-*lo*-ny, John had explained, dated from at least as long ago as the twelfth century, and is entirely local to the county of Angus. Its meaning derives from a hill called Lony, about six miles northwest of the Guynd, which the family claimed as their own back in the Middle Ages. *Ouchter* is Gaelic for "over" or "on top of." So all the Ouchterlonys and the many variations on the name since (Ochterloney, Auchterlonie, Uchterlony, etc.) descend from this ancient clan on the hill.

By now the Ouchterlonys are spread far and wide. John mentioned in particular a large exodus to Sweden in the eighteenth century. By the late nineteenth century the last heir to the Guynd had to reach several branches side-ways across the family tree to appoint his fourth cousin once removed—John's grandfather—as the last hope of keeping the family name alive in Angus. From the obitu-aries pasted in the latter pages of the diary I gathered that although the Colonel was new to the area (he had been called up from Devonshire) he quickly made his presence warmly felt with the local population both humble and grand. Gregarious, civic-minded, the exemplary military man, he understood that protecting the family name was implicit in his stroke of fate and immediately set about preparing the ground for his son and heir.

In the Colonel's steady, forward-slanting hand, this faithfully kept diary of events of family and estate revealed a surprising fact, that John's father, Thomas, was not the firstborn son (the Colonel had six children altogether; first came Nora, then the three boys, John—known as Jack—Thomas, and Guy, and finally the twins, Arthur and Mary) and had therefore not grown up expecting to take over the Guynd.

I saved my discovery to discuss with John over dinner that evening. "Did you know," I began, "that your father was the *second* son?"

"Well let's see, Nora was the eldest . . ."

"Then John, known as Jack," I went on.

"Uncle Jack, right. I never knew him," said John, grinding a carpet of pepper over his haddock. "So he was the first son? I guess he was."

It was clear that John had either never known this fact or forgotten it, obscured as it was in the dark corners of the mind where the might-have-beens or what-ifs lurk and are best left undisturbed. For the biographer, on the other hand, this was the stuff of a story, a key that turns a dutiful list of dates into a human drama. Was being the second son at the core of Tom's disturbing jealousy toward his own firstborn?

"Maybe," said John mildly, not quite as entranced with my research as I thought he might be.

Armed with this narrative handle, I ventured further the following day into the Colonel's diary, where it became increasingly clear that Tom was raised in the shadow of his older brother Jack, the heir apparent. So this was the proud young man in the uniform with his long

Ouchterlony face, straight sharp nose, and hooded eyes, who looked resolutely past my shoulder out of the picture frame in the cellar. This was the man whose military medals were nestled in fitted purple velvet, snapped shut in a leather case and covered with dust. This was the boy whose glowing reports from Woolwich Academy dropped in my lap from the pages of his father's diary. Here he was in the picture album, fourth from the left, dressed up as Bonnie Prince Charlie for an amateur theatrical by the lake.

A gold engraved invitation to luncheon announced Jack's coming of age in 1906. A marquee was erected on the lawn; floral archways decorated the drives. In Jack's honor a young spruce tree was ceremoniously planted in a conspicuous spot along the edge of the lakeside lawn. Dinner and dancing for the tenant farmers and local shop-keepers was followed by a grand evening party for the gentry. A printed program of toasts ensured that the right things were said by the right people, and all raised their glasses to the young lieutenant and future laird of the Guynd.

First however he would have to prove himself in the larger world. Stationed in West Africa with the Royal Engineers, Jack was credited with directing the construction of the Great Ashantee Road in Ghana, which many believed was a monument of engineering skill among the finest in West Africa, and which earned him the title of major. In 1915, by then a married man with a child on the way, Jack felt that his duty was at the Western Front in

France. On June 17, 1917, he was killed in action near Ypres. His commanding officer wrote a three-page letter to the family describing his death, explaining exactly how and where it happened, assuring them that it was quick, and concluding that he himself had lost "one of the best officers I have ever known."

Here in Britain, couples have long been advised to produce, if possible, a second son, just in case of an untimely death of the male heir due to war or fatal illness. They call it "the heir and the spare."

In America spare can mean stark or plain. In Britain it more often means extra. They speak, for instance, of the "spare room," rather than the more inviting "guest room" we offer in America. Sure enough, our spare room at the Guynd looked quite spare, in the American sense, even though it was painted pink and contained more spare chairs, in the British sense, than anyone could think of reasons to sit in during a week's stay. John always emphasized the wisdom of having a spare two or three tins of tomatoes in the kitchen cupboard, anticipating a small meteorological disaster, or a spare and hungry cousin showing up unannounced. The number of spare parts John has raided from other people's castoffs and collected in his workshop would take more than a lifetime to employ. To an urban American used to instant access to everything this may seem a bizarre and unnecessary act of hoarding, but in Scotland the primal urge to store away for the afterlife is a hangover from leaner, meaner times. Did this represent a faith—or, on the contrary, a lack of faith—in the future?

It was John's mother who taught him to save. I discovered her string collection in an upstairs cupboard, of various lengths and strengths, neatly looped and tied and ready to use again. In the kitchen I opened a drawer one day to find it brimming with candle ends; the idea, John explained, was to melt them down and mold them into new candles, someday. Behind the jars of honey and jam on a high shelf I discovered half a dozen bottles of home-made raspberry vinegar, conscientiously labeled in his mother's careful hand with the date, 1960.

"Nineteen-sixty?"

"Oh, that shouldn't make any difference," said John. "Vinegar lasts forever, I should think."

He should think. So why did somebody bother to put a date on it?

"What about this black currant jam? It's crystallized! Couldn't we throw it out?" John hesitated, suggesting that we might give it to someone who keeps bees, though he couldn't think who just then.

"What about the egg boxes, that arcing tower of them on the back stairs? Who are we saving those for?"

"Someone who keeps ducks or geese or hens will need those, you wait and see. We used to have hens here at the Guynd. Freshly laid eggs every day."

I was perhaps better equipped than many Americans to understand this kitchen clutter, as my mother was something of a saver too. In her kitchen she always kept a drawer full of washed, ironed, and neatly folded aluminum foil. Her homemade soups always originated with the water she'd drained from cooking the vegetables. She saved the empty butter wrappers in the fridge to grease the pans, though she never baked a cake. My mother and John's—the British-born, living through the Depression and wartime—would have understood each other's domestic habits perfectly. Never waste. Always have something to spare.

But how, I wondered, did it feel to grow up knowing that you were a spare child? As the second son you are part of a plan for disaster. You are a shadow figure, hovering, ready for the part you may never get, knowing that getting it would be at the cost of a tragedy that would mark your brother a greater hero than you for all time. What John's father felt about it growing up we can only guess, but by the time the responsibility of the Guynd fell to him at the Colonel's death in 1922, he did not look like a lucky man.

By the mid-1920s "the estate was not washing her face," as Tom put it to his trustees many years later. A growing influx of foreign goods from abroad had seriously depressed farm rents; landowners could no longer depend upon that income to cover the cost of running the house and estate. Furthermore, with the new Labour government in power there were the ever rising death duties to pay. Only the very rich (most often those whose income came from industry, not agriculture) could afford to pay them, while the merely land-rich were forced to sell off significant assets. The Ouchterlonys, I gathered, were among the latter. British confidence in land ownership as an incomparable security was fast eroding. The very spirit of the class system that held these places intact was threatened by the loss of so many eldest sons in the Great War.

Tom meanwhile, still a bachelor, had grown accustomed to the peripatetic life of a naval officer and found pleasure in the camaraderie of men at sea. His parents were both dead, and so were two of his brothers—Jack, the war hero, and Guy, who had moved to Canada and married, then drowned in Lake Ontario in a heroic and unsuccessful attempt to rescue two children from the same fate. Meanwhile the youngest brother, Arthur, would never recover from shell shock following two months in the trenches in 1917.

Tom's sisters had fared somewhat better. Nora was married to a judge and living in London. Only Mary, Arthur's twin, remained at the Guynd. A freckled, ginger-haired maiden in her early thirties, she had nursed their father through his last illness. Now down to two house servants from the nine she had grown up with, Mary was otherwise alone in this thirty-two-room house.

Little effort had been put into the estate for ten years. The triumphant days of Jack's coming of age—of garlands and marquees, tea parties on the lawn and theatricals by the lake—was the Guynd of the past, evaporating in the mist of Edwardian nostalgia. Its future, as far as Tom was concerned, was looking highly questionable. And he was not alone. During the interwar years such places were held in contempt as old, ugly, extravagant, and emptied of their purpose.

In the glass-fronted bookcase on the upstairs landing, I found the books John's mother had collected over the years on country houses and castles, gardens and land-scapes—guidebooks, handbooks, and opulent picture books, all expounding on the grand and glorious traditions of which the Guynd was part. By far the most resonant for me was a volume called *The Destruction of the Country House*, a heavy paperback catalogue crowded with black-and-white photographs of abandoned stately piles. This was the battle cry of the 1970s preservationists led by Roy Strong, then director of the Victoria and Albert Museum, with a highly publicized exhibition. With cold accuracy the book is a roll call of some nine hundred houses and castles that had met the wrecking ball in the first half of the twentieth century. Like Walker Evans's photographs of abandoned plantation houses in Louisiana in the 1930s, it was deeply depressing, all despair and regret, haunted by an irredeemable past and despairing of the future.

Yet somehow this awful book was a comfort to me. If it had been that difficult to hang on, the Guynd wasn't doing so badly after all. It had actually made it through the most challenging years of the century safely to the other side. That the house still remained in the family who built it, while others had become hotels or schools or retirement homes, if they stood at all, was nothing short of a miracle. This was not the time to feel ashamed of its chipped capitals and missing balusters, its potholed drives and over-grown garden.

For those with vivid memories of its glory days,

though, it must have been another matter altogether to feel it slipping out of control. A newspaper clipping in the Colonel's diary (taken over by the faithful Mary) tells that in April 1924, the Guynd was advertised "For Sale by Private Bargain . . . about 950 acres . . . Mansion House . . . situated in extensive policies, 5 public, 10 bed and dressing rooms . . . 4 arable farms and a Home Farm."

"John," I ventured one evening, "did you know that your father put the Guynd on the market in 1924?"

"Not a good market, I guess," said John.

A year and a half later no buyer had emerged and the house and grounds were withdrawn from the market, though some farmland and furniture were sold off to cover death duties. Mary advertised for paying guests and kept the house running, hosting the occasional visits from family and friends. Finally Mary moved to a cottage in the neighboring county of Perthshire when full-time renters came forward to take on the Guynd. The Geoffrey Coxes, a Dundee family who had made their fortune in the jute business (Dundee, they say, owes its onetime prosperity to the three J's: jute, jam, and journalism), had the money and fresh initiative to bring the mansion house up to modern standards, particularly the onerous task of installing central heating and modern plumbing. Many much larger country houses were not so fortunate, which spelled their ruin. It is fair to say that the Coxes, though they paid a bargain rent for the Guynd of 350 pounds a year, were its savior in those precarious times.

Meanwhile Tom was stationed all over Britain with

the navy. Finally, aged forty-five, his heart was won by a young woman more than twenty years his junior, the witty and wellborn Doreen Mary Joan Lloyd (this was the point at which my family and John's converged; she was "Aunt Dodie" to my cousins in Vancouver). Doreen was the eldest daughter of a respectable English-Welsh family from Wimbledon Common. Her father was a London lawyer and among the founders of the world-renowned tennis tournament. Her sister Joy remembers that Dodie was "head over heels" in love with Tom. Though her parents were anxious about the wisdom of their daughter's choice of so much older a man, there was nothing to be done. Tom and his "darling wee girl," as he fondly addressed her, were married in 1935 and settled near the Guynd in a rented house, where my John was born less than two years later.

For John growing up, visits to the Guynd were enchanted. The promise that it would someday be theirs again—entirely theirs—shone like a pot of gold. All that space! Oceans of lawn, caves of rhododendrons, and paths through the woods, where huge beech trees with their smooth gray trunks rose to a fluttering green canopy. There was the lake, and the walled garden, abundant with sweet-smelling flowers and vegetables, and the *burn* to paddle his feet or follow along its gurgling way.

When war broke out again in Europe, John's life as a child changed little except he might have noticed that his father had disappeared. Tom, having just settled into married retirement, was posted as British consul in Esbjerg. In

April 1940, the Nazis invaded Copenhagen. Tom missed his train back to Esbjerg, being embroiled on the platform in an argument with the conductor—so the story goes— and was taken prisoner. Exactly a week before, his second son, Angus, was born.

I found Tom's wartime letters in the library desk, tied in neat bundles, every one stamped CENSORED in bold black type. Searching for clues to the pain he allegedly suffered for some months in solitary confinement, I learned only that he was put to work raising vegetables for the Germans. Boredom was the only form of suffering his letters expressed. "If there was never anything to tell you about my extraordinarily dull life in Esbjerg," he wrote to Doreen from Germany, "I'm afraid there will be even less I can write from here." His letters consist of requests for luxuries such as Players cigarettes and dried figs, necessities like gardening shorts and hats, and Penguin paperbacks. Though a somewhat futile gesture, he also attempted to direct his wife as to the management of affairs at home.

Soon after Tom's arrest the Guynd, at Doreen's consent, was requisitioned as a barrack for the Women's Royal Navy, familiarly known as "the Wrens." As many as fifty women moved into the house, sleeping in rows of cots covering the floor of the dining room, the library, and the drawing room, with the petty officers in more spacious comfort in the upstairs bedrooms. Later, in 1942, the house became a residence for the head of the nearby naval base—the Admiral—his family, and five male servants.

All in all the Guynd was spared the kind of destruction that many similar and much larger houses suffered during the war. ("Wonderful old place in its way," said the Quartering Commandant as he stood before the castle in *Brideshead Revisited*, preparing to take it over. "Pity to knock it about too much.") Even so, the Guynd's recovery was painfully slow.

That first summer I spent there, nearly fifty years after the war ended, it still felt like a place caught in a transition between institution and home. Stripped down for the heavy wear and tear of wartime, it had never regained the intimacy of family life. Though women are known to be gentler tenants than men, signs of their occupation remained. Some of the windows bore the faint tape marks left from blacking them out every evening at dusk. The architrave in the library was pockmarked with holes where the Wrens had inserted sturdy clothes hooks. Inside the dining room cupboard the shelves, then used for bed linen, bore the humorous names they had given to their dormitories—"Shangri-la," "Sleepy Hollow," and "Davy Jones' Locker." More than anything else it was the dreary brown linoleum, which covered the floors of every room in the house, that seemed to me such a stark reminder of the hordes of indifferent transients tramping through the place. I longed to tear it out.

"Good quality stuff," John replied. He'd lived with it so long he hardly noticed it was there. "Military standard, after all." This was known as high praise in his family. "Just look how well it's lasted!"

Anything that lasts, in other words, earns its right to stay. With a philosophy like that, no wonder the house was so depressing. Someone had to break the mold, and that someone appeared to be me. One day I lifted a corner of the dreaded stuff and discovered that it wasn't even tacked to the floor. The job of lifting it out of the dining room would take an afternoon. I accosted John at lunchtime. "The stuff isn't even tacked to the floor! Why can't we just roll it up?"

"Did you notice the state of the floors underneath?" John asked rhetorically.

"So what! Anything's better than that lino!"

That very afternoon we moved all the furniture into the hall and rolled up the several lengths of linoleum that covered the floor. John carefully measured each piece, and then tied them up with string so they could be neatly transported to the farm buildings for some as yet unimagined future use. Then we rolled up the old Turkish carpet in the hall, exposing smooth gray flagstones, and moved a large circular veneered table into the middle of the floor as a centerpiece—a surface on which to drop the keys or the mail, or to place a cheerful vase of fresh flowers. There was nothing to it. Only that one thing inevitably would lead to another.

And so it did. The dust was disturbed and there was no turning back.

THREE

Winter Light

. . .

I RETURNED TO THE GUYND IN MID-OCTOBER THAT same year. Arriving first in London, I helped John pack up his flat in Kensington as he was giving up his lease. Now that his attention was turning more fully to the Guynd, and our city life favored New York, the London flat was not going to see enough use to be worth the expense of renting it. John's London life, I felt anyway, had not been much more than a lingering postponement of his responsibilities at the Guynd. His London friends, gathering regularly for a pint or two or three at Churchill's pub, seemed to regard his Scottish background as not much more than the uproarious stuff of English comedy, and John as the uprooted eccentric in their midst. His Scottish friends, on the other hand, went way back; they understood where he came from, and they actually cared.

In my spare time I had discovered the delights of the Fulham Road with its posh decorator's shops like Colefax and Fowler, and Farrow and Ball, which unlike their American counterparts are open to the general public. I browsed the racks of fabric and wallpaper and compared paint swatches in earthy colors they deemed historic such as Georgian Green, Eating Room Red, Hay, and Drab. At the prospect of waking up in that dismal master bedroom at the Guynd, I collected a bundle of wallpaper samples in bright floral motifs. In the shorter run, a decent kitchen knife and a cheerful Italian ceramic salad bowl would make all the difference. Then we were off on the long drive to the Guynd, where I would resume writing and get a feel for the rapidly darkening days of late fall in Scotland. My mother, who knew firsthand about the limits of British-style central heating, had shipped over a Vermont Castings wood stove for my study. We met it at the freight department of the Edinburgh airport and somehow John managed to fit the entire bulk of its 110 kilos into the back of our new, secondhand Ford Escort, which meant that Foxy had to sit on my lap.

It was cold but the countryside was deceptively green. As we drove over the gently whipped hills of Fife in the thinning light we noted that the winter wheat the farmers planted in August was just beginning to sprout like grass, It was Halloween, but I was not expecting to see any sign of the occasion in Scotland.

On our way north through Kinross we dropped in on the Adams, old friends of John's whose ancestors were the Adam Brothers of architectural fame. Like John, Keith Adam and his wife, Elizabeth, were struggling to hang on to their oversized family pile. Blair Adam, as the house is called, can be spied from the highway. Just after we passed the sign for Kelty, John told me where to look for it. Perched high on a hill, its roofline is just visible for a moment behind a thick grove of trees. Leaving the highway we traveled along a narrow bumpy road that at some indecipherable point became a private drive, reaching the entrance to the house as we rounded a hairpin turn at the top of a steep rise. At least twice as big as the Guynd, Blair Adam was also a great deal more eccentric. "It's been added on to at various stages," John explained at our approach. And propped up at various others, I judged from the row of buttresses flanking the east wall.

Keith welcomed us into a small front hall at the east end of the house, then on through to an enormous room— as big as a ballroom—which connects the two wings of the house and which they call, with typical Scottish understatement, "the corridor." Yet the scale of this room was made comfortable by the presence of large sofas and armchairs, antique tables, and faded Oriental carpets; it had that layered, cluttered, tea-stained effect—what the French call *le désordre britannique*, and which somehow the Guynd had managed to get wrong. John remembered visiting Blair Adam as a child when on a rainy afternoon buckets were dotted here and there on the floor catching leaks from the roof, and on one occasion when a piece of the dining room ceiling fell into somebody's soup plate. The roof actually caved in over a section of the house when Keith was about three years old, and eventually it succumbed to ruin. At that point in the century, when the idea of living in a grand house became synonymous with roughing it, and frugality with good breeding, a generation was born that took such mishaps for granted, and their mission was clear. Slowly but surely Keith and Elizabeth would recapture whatever they could of the place for the next generation of Adams.

In the corridor that night all was dark except for the light from a huge crackling fire. Katherine and Louisa, the Adams' twin twelve-year-old daughters, were hosting a Halloween party. About eight or ten girls sat in a circle in the glow of the fire playing word games, anticipating the terrors to come. Suddenly two figures (the twins' older brother and cousin) emerged through a far door in the shadows, hunched over in overcoats and cackling like ghouls. One by one the girls were plucked out of the circle, blindfolded, and led through the "chamber of horrors" (the larger of the two dining rooms), where the boys, holding each one firmly to their delighted screams, directed their feet over broken skeletons (croquet mallets), dipped their hands in raw intestines (cold spaghetti) and witch's blood (tepid soup), and finally hustled them outside and into the hayloft for ghost stories and pizza.

Keith's twin sister, Rita, was also there that evening. An old girlfriend of John's, she was frankly fascinated to meet me, wondering, I supposed, if I was some airheaded American with stars in her eyes or whether I really had any idea what I was in for. She sat in a generous armchair with her aging English pointer, Jonah, dozing in her lap, fixed me with her mischievous sharp hazel eyes, and started to test me for reactions. *"Awfully* gloomy house, the Guynd, isn't it?" I answered her with my eyes and she let loose a laugh like a machine gun, and we began then and there to bond in sympathy for living with John, the one having given up (why *had* Rita given up, I wondered, when clearly she and John had so much in common?), the other fresh to the task. "Tell me," she asked in a loud whisper, "is there still an egg timer by the telephone?"

Rita and her family reminded me of families I knew back home—history-minded, humorous, and unaffected, relaxed amid their inherited surroundings. Like good old Bostonians they were obviously concerned but not anxious about the imperfect state of Blair Adam. Furthermore, for me there was an added connection to the Adam family. My own great-great-great grandfather Bonomi (the one whose drawing hung in our dining room) had begun his architectural career as a draftsman for Robert Adam.

"What did you say his name was? Bo*n*omi?" asked Keith. "No, I've never heard of him. I wonder if we could find his name in one of these volumes," and he began searching the library shelves.

"Robert Adam met my ancestor in Rome," I explained. "Apparently he was impressed with Bonomi's draftsmanship and his intimate knowledge of classical Rome, so he imported him to London, I think about 1760-something."

"Of course there were a great many draftsmen, or *decorators,* in the firm," Keith said in defense of his ignorance, leafing through a large leather volume.

"Bonomi," I felt I had to say, "went on to establish his own practice as an architect. Have you ever heard of Rosneath Castle? He designed it for the Duke of Argyll." (Unfortunately, Rosneath also happened to be one of the doomed piles in Roy Strong's catalogue of destroyed country houses.)

What would the architect and his draftsman think of us now, of their various descendants meeting by sheer coincidence, caught by surprise in a transatlantic alliance of country house maintenance in the late twentieth century? And had we met in London, say, or New York, would the meeting have anything like the same resonance, the same tangibility for that historic connection, that it had in the architect's library in the kingdom of Fife?

BACK AT THE GUYND the autumn sunlight slanted across the rooms, raising the specter of dust on every surface, illuminating the chipped cornice or cracks in the wall paint. The ironwork of the banister cast a sharp-focus shadow on the wall, crisp as the echo of a voice across a frozen field. Then the sun disappeared suddenly behind a cloud, the light was too dim to remember where to dust, and it didn't matter anyway.

The long days of a northern summer were now traded in for the short days of a northern winter, and I wondered if we had invested heavily enough in the daylight hours that were once abundant and now so scarce. Some mornings we would awake to see a coat of hoarfrost over the green fields. Matted brown leaves, their veins painted silver, sparkled and crunched under my Wellington boots as Foxy led me along the open roads. The "beasts" were still in the fields, but soon would be moved to their farmers' sheds for the winter. From across the field the house stood starkly; the windows like sheets of silver winked back at me as the sun hit them sideways. The strange thing was that the frost would still be there just the same in the afternoon; the sun never rose high enough to burn it off. It just hung there, at half-mast, and then went down! This was a twilight world.

There were various residential tenants in place, which helped to tone down the effect of gathering winter isolation. Stephen, the artist, lived downstairs in the West flat. A graduate of the Glasgow School of Art, Stephen painted dark, foreboding landscapes in a style that John facetiously called the Scottish School of Gloom, and which clearly drew much of their inspiration from the Guynd. He lived with his German girlfriend, Ilka, and their one-year-old daughter, Gwen. Stephen was frankly delighted to find in me someone with whom he could talk seriously about Max Beckmann. As for me, the idea of making a studio visit under our very own roof was well beyond my expectations.

"Stephen prices his paintings by the yard," explained John, rather derisively, I thought, even if it was true. Paintings weren't the same as cornices, please.

"A large painting is a more ambitious undertaking than a small one," I told him, a mite stiffly.

In the East flat lived another young couple. David had

a secondhand furniture business in Dundee, and his wife, Jill, was a vet. The entrance lodge at the front gate was occupied by a young bachelor named Robert, who worked for the telephone company. Living alone at the edge of the estate, he hardly ever crossed our path. There was a complex of farm buildings half a mile down the East drive at the back gate, which included an L-shaped steading, a U-shaped piggery, and a row of three attached cottages, at the time empty but one, which housed an old widower named Fayerweather. A passionate gardener, Fayerweather single-handedly managed a large vegetable patch behind the old piggery. We'd encounter him, a stooped white-haired man, harvesting the last of the summer crop and he would invite us to help ourselves to the brussels sprouts, whenever. And he told me where to look for the "wee wild orchid" that grew near the dam. Finally there was a mysterious old couple, the Fishers, living in a grim little house near the farm, which used to be the residence of the overseer. We could tell that the Fishers were home from the coal smoke curling out of their chimney, but we hardly ever saw a figure emerge from that house to find his or her way through the thicket of weeds and past the graveyard of half a dozen or so dead automobiles that surrounded it.

Upstairs in my study John inserted a stainless steel coil of chimney liner through the opening in the fireplace to the roof and hooked up our brand-new woodstove. Matte black with sturdy old-fashioned lines and a window through which you could see the silent waving of orange flames, warming the room through and through, my stove was more comforting to me than an open fire. During the shortening days of late fall I escaped into my work, my trap door back to America.

We still observed the "tea ritual," as John drolly referred to it, every afternoon at about five o'clock, but we no longer trekked with the trolley out to the drawing room, which was too cold for comfort, its drafts now isolated behind a heavy curtain in the library. We gave up the silver teapot for the fat white kitchen model, more or less permanently dressed in its crocheted tea cozy that looked like an old ski hat out of the Lost and Found. Forget about the bone china cups and saucers; one of the variety of chipped mugs out of the kitchen cupboard would do. But the tea itself, in spite of its ritual being trimmed down to a kind of stand-up affair, was as good as ever. It seemed there was always something more to learn about making a "proper pot of tea." Like pouring the boiling water into the pot from a height, "to help it aerate," explained John. Or, one should "always mix the Lapsang Suchong with an equal amount of Bengal, to tone down the smoky taste." And then, as I poured out the first cup, "How long has it been steeping?" He always checked; and, "Did you remember to give it a stir?"

This ample supply of loose tea came from an old-fashioned emporium in Dundee called Braithwaite's, which stood in the same location on Castle Street where it had opened a hundred years ago. Miraculously, twentieth-century progress had left Braithwaite's in its wake. An attendant in a red smock would appear behind the counter at the jingle of the bell on the door as we entered its scented sanctuary. The two-foot-high japanned tin canisters still lined the upper shelves labeled China, Darjeeling, Earl Grey, Lapsang Suchong, and Bengal. Lifting down the great tin of Darjeeling from above, the attendant's experienced hand would tap the nearly exact quantity into the shiny brass scales on the counter, and then with a series of counterweights tap a little more until the scales hovered in perfect balance. "Anything else? Two pounds fifty, please!" was the cost of this performance, and with a quick exchange of coins and the *thrrinng!* of the old cash register we were out the door and into the twentieth century again.

These were the simple comforts of country life in winter, I thought to myself as we climbed the gray roads out of the depths of not-very-bonnie Dundee, making our way past faceless housing blocks, where people whose lives I would never know carried on day to day, their windows decked out in frilly curtains and lit up now in the yellow glow of electric lights as dusk fell. We sped past supermarkets, industrial estates, and around so many roundabouts that I thought we were going in circles until we finally made the turn onto the back road that leads eleven miles to the front gate of the Guynd. Home in time for tea.

Late November closed in on us. At sunset, about three-thirty in the afternoon, we went around the house closing all the interior shutters against the cold. The sun, if it had appeared at all, would have done what it could to warm the rooms. It was still too soon to fire up the furnace

(never before the first of December, goes the local con-
vention. And off by the first of March, as John explained
was the custom of his friends at Dunninald, another large
house nearby, suggesting strongly that we too would be
following the same sensible, ritual logic. Do you think this
is America?) Once the heat was on, the small radiators had
only from four o' clock in the afternoon until midnight to
do their job.

The kitchen was the coldest room in the house. I
pared down my cooking efforts from the stews and salads
I had enjoyed concocting in the summer to the bare mini-
mum on a wintry evening. A quick dash into the kitchen
to shove a frozen breaded chicken cutlet into the little
portable electric oven, then back to the fireside, or stove-
side, as fast as I could go. "Close the door!" John reminded me every time I left a room, so as not to let the precious
heat escape into the passages.

"We are huddled up in my study most evenings now,"
I wrote to my mother, "around the Vermont Castings
woodstove. The house has become a huge empty shell we
walk through in search of this or that."

I switched on the electric blanket about an hour before
going to bed. Then, turning it off again (under John's
strict instructions), I sank into the dry pool of warmth.
Just as the pool was beginning to ebb, John would arrive
in the dark like a great human radiator beside me.
Mornings, I was greeted by Foxy's wet nose breathing
near my face, accompanied by a vigorous wagging of a tail
as I began to stir. It took all my strength of character to get

out of bed and don my three or four layers of insulation. Once dressed, I could hardly wait for an excuse to jump into the car, turn on the heat, and drive away! Off to the bright lights of the Safeway in Arbroath, to the heated aisles of packaged food and fresh vegetables from Africa, and perhaps afterward a cup of coffee with Angus's ex-wife Alison, who lived alone in her semidetached bungalow on the outskirts of town.

Alison had grown up in an unheated shooting lodge high in the hills of windswept Aberdeenshire, had subsequently raised her own family in a damp basement flat at the Guynd, and was now as happy as she could be in her tidy little suburban stucco, easy to clean and heat. There she would be in her apron and rubber gloves, rolling up her sleeves to wipe a few stray crumbs from her immaculate countertop, or placing a carefully constructed pudding into the right drawer of her enormous freezer chest. I always took my shoes off so as not to tread on her mauve carpet, and I left the dog in the car. Alison was all sympathy and cheerful banter about the practical matters of life, of cooking and shopping. But our favorite subject by far was family. I quickly discovered what valuable insight she could provide into the native Ouchterlony character. And since she revealed not a shred of envy for my taking on the big house, nor lingering resentment that she had not, our relationship was remarkably uncomplicated from the start. "I so admire you," she said. "I never could have taken on a house like that."

"Maybe I just don't know any better," I replied.

Alison was charmed by my daring, and I by her modesty and her candor. She would share from her fund of memories and insights into recent family life at the Guynd and the mysterious past of earlier generations of Ouchterlonys. We compared the two brothers—John and Angus—their characters, their histories, who resembled which parent in what way. "They're as different as chalk and cheese," said Alison, "and I'm afraid they were not very good friends." Angus, with his ginger hair, was supposed to be lighthearted; John was dark, and seemed deeper. Angus was the sporty one, John the intellectual. Angus moved fast and impulsively, John cautiously and with deliberation. Angus was a spendthrift, John was frugal. Angus threw things away, and John, furious, rescued them. Instead of finding in the other a useful complement, their differing natures grated on each other and brought out their worst and most competitive behavior, each vying, as brothers will, for supremacy.

Posing in their kilts for the lady photographer who toured the county once a year with her 8 x 10 view camera, black cloth, and tripod, Angus, aged about nine, appears to be looking up at his older brother with great respect. Perhaps this was just for the picture, or perhaps there was a time, barely remembered by anyone, when they were friends. The more I learned, the more I wondered which of the two was the prodigal son, or whether they simply took turns at it. Angus, who eventually fled to Canada, leaving his wife and children? Or John, who took off at a younger age, leaving job and career to follow the trail of his curiosity and to get as far away as possible from the fate that was already spelled out for him? Both rebelled in their own way from the strictness of their upbringing, and neither was granted the prodigal son's warm welcome home by their father. "I suspect he was terribly jealous of his boys," Alison ventured. "Mother-in-law didn't make it any easier, to my mind."

BY THE TIME John's father was released by the Germans and returned to Scotland at the end of the war, John hardly remembered him; Angus had never met him, and their mother, Tom's "darling wee girl," had grown accustomed to being in charge. Tom was a changed man—two world wars had left their indelible scars on his psyche—and the world was a changed place. It was too painful and too daunting a prospect to recapture the Guynd of the past. Restoring it to the image of his childhood was inconceivable. Anyway, he might have figured, it never had his name on it. Survivor's guilt dogged him. Two brothers had died tragically, heroically, while he had spent the war years watering tomato plants for the enemy.

Doreen was anxious to return the house to the family, but for a few years Tom—the Commander—was satisfied to establish a flat in the West end of the basement, leaving the Admiral upstairs presiding over the principal rooms. Perhaps this was to drive home the point of wartime pecking order, that military duty took precedence over family life. Perhaps it had something to do with Tom's having spent three years in command of a submarine during the

First World War. Did being underneath give him a feeling of safety, or of subterfuge, which he had developed an affinity for? Whatever the reasons, faced with Tom's inertia it took many months of Doreen's persistent prodding to get the Admiral's family moved out of the house and her own upstairs. From then on, as John recalls, his father spent a good deal of his time sequestered in the library in front of the TV with the shutters closed, surrounded by a barricade of club armchairs.

As John remembered him, his father didn't seem to have a past or a family worth talking about. He was moody, irritable, and intimidating. Every morning the boys had to stand at attention at the foot of his bed, waiting for their orders. Tom spent the morning in the desultory business of his new raison d'être as Secretary of the Shipwrecked Mariner's Society. At precisely one o'clock he would begin to stir, demanding of his wife, "Where's lunch?" Commanding his two or three estate workers toward the planting of trees, the raising of pigs, the mending of fences and gates, and, in a more energetic mood, reprimanding the estate managers, he tried to recapture the sense of power he had felt in his finest hours in the navy. But there was no real enemy to be vanquished, no territory to conquer. Often Tom would take to his bed and not be available for days. It was well known that his marriage was unhappy, and that his two boys were afraid of him. Even in later years, when the boys were grown up, Alison recalls that when the Commander appeared "everyone else would sort of scatter."

As the boys grew up and were packed off to boarding school, Tom and Doreen led increasingly separate lives, each claiming his and her own end of the house. Doreen would retire to her sewing room upstairs to play her accordion to herself. Tom loathed the sound of it. Perhaps he suspected that her love of the instrument had something to do with one of those dashing Polish army refugees that so cheered the lonely wives of Angus County during the war, with their shiny black riding boots and their fast-swinging mazurkas. Tom had no interest in dancing of any kind.

By the 1960s, I learned from a letter Tom wrote to his middle-aged Canadian nephew, he had concluded that his wife was "a townie," and that his two teenage boys evinced no real interest in the country. Occasionally he could persuade Angus to go shooting with him, which gave him a ray of hope, but mostly, he complained, "parties, cinema, country dancing, pretty well contain their thoughts, except when the lake is frozen." If Tom had ever felt the same way in his youth he had long since forgotten it.

John's parents also cultivated different sets of friends, Doreen's among the upper-crust county families, while Tom was more comfortable with the local farmers and the transient military population, always in good supply from the nearby naval air base. One such witness to this situation, a retired naval officer, came to call on us one day in the summer, interested to see the old Guynd again. John instantly disappeared, leaving me to receive the man's candid recollections. "The Commander liked me," he told me, adding jovially, "which of course made me rather unpopular with the rest of the family."

More than one family acquaintance has told me about having been invited to the Guynd for tea, and then being sent away when the knock at the door was met by the Commander, who knew nothing of their invitation. Likewise, Doreen was known to give a cool reception to anyone looking for Tom. She was not expected to participate in his dinner or lunch parties, nor did she care to, to hear Tom telling the same old war stories and his favorite off-color jokes. One was either his friend or hers, and whichever one was, it was almost impossible not to take sides in the battle over how the Guynd should best be managed or—God forbid—enjoyed.

Clearly, I realized, it was impossible for Doreen to make the house as beautiful as she would have liked it to be, as beautiful as it deserved to be, without Tom's support. Nothing like the upheaval I had already caused by raising the linoleum would ever have been allowed, even though it wouldn't have cost them anything. A fresh coat of paint would have been welcome everywhere but that was obviously out of the question. Soft furnishings, it seems, were Doreen's only outlet. Even so, the curtains she had made were nervously cut to the narrowest margin, not quite meeting in the middle when they were drawn, and the pelmets were too shallow for those high, generous windows.

The stingy little lamps, the walls in need of paint Tom could abide even if Doreen could not. The feared and isolated patriarch complained to his trustees of his family's "soaring expenditure in electricity, due to staggered meals, and their own private sitting room." He was known to have cut off the hot water supply when he thought his family was being extravagant with it. Yet a striking double standard was not hard to see in Tom's definition of luxury. He bought a showy two-seater open-top Lee Francis motor car, which is remembered to this day by certain elderly residents of Arbroath. And there was no surer way to impress the county folk with his youthful vigor and enterprise than a heated outdoor swimming pool, which Tom decided he could afford to build in the early 1960s. Furthermore, there was no more public a rejection of his wife's desires than to smother her lawn tennis court in the process—the ultimate insult to her Wimbledon childhood.

Tom played his new social asset to the hilt, inviting everybody for a swim. While he basked in his superficial popularity, flirting with the girls in their bathing suits, exhibiting his own remarkably lean figure afloat in an inner tube, Doreen hurried up and down the stairs for extra towels and fretted as children left their wet footprints all over the front hall on their way to the loo. John, having just earned his engineering degree in Aberdeen, outwardly criticized the pool's poorly designed drainage system and privately fumed over his father's disregard for his expertise. Alison worried about the safety of her three small children, as she and Angus then resided in the basement flat. Sure enough, one day little Pete, aged four, was discovered floating head down in the pool; the gardener rescued him just in time.

Some of her friends considered Doreen a saint not to have deserted Tom. Certainly she went to church every Sunday, attended religious retreats in foreign countries, and prayed a lot at home. A prie-dieu in the corner of the passage upstairs, upholstered in rough brown stuff, faced a religious icon, which I quietly banished to a drawer. Endurance, one friend told me, was Doreen's great strength. Her long trial ended in 1971 when Tom died suddenly of a stroke. Wrote the headmaster of Fort Augustus, the Catholic monastery where the boys had gone to school, "He has finally gone to that place above the dark cloud that hung over him and made him an unhappy man."

The dark cloud that had hung over the Guynd began to lift after Tom died. His family was free to make decisions, to go about its business, without the constant fear of his criticism. But Doreen had by then lost her energy to make the house beautiful. It lingered in a state of postwar semi-recovery, as she eventually moved downstairs to Tom's office, no longer having the strength to climb the stairs. This spacious room with a window to the floor gave Foxy a place to doze in the sun or prick up her sharp ears and announce a visitor approaching the front door. John fitted a stove into the fireplace so that his mother could keep herself warm in winter. With Foxy she took walks in the woods to escape the icy winds of the open road. In April she decamped for Portugal where she shared a house with friends. Back at the Guynd in summer, she spent the last two weeks of every June faithfully watching the Wimbledon finals. John remembers the *pop, pop, pop* of the tennis balls emanating day after day from behind the closed doors of the darkened library.

That first fall I spent at the Guynd, Doreen's freshly dry-cleaned tartan skirts still hung in the cupboard, her feathered hats perched on the shelf swathed in tissue paper. In the drawer of a little Pembroke table I sorted through her powders and pills, creams and lipsticks, and as I tossed them one by one into the wastebasket I wondered what it was like to live here all alone. Her diaries, little leather books each no bigger than the palm of my hand, stuffed to the back of a desk drawer, accounted for thirty-six years of marriage, every day of it recorded briefly in pencil, as another test of her endurance passed into night. "Rain, walked with Foxy in the woods, T. not speaking to J."

"Had she been ailing for a long time before she died?" I asked John.

"Not at all. She was out at the theater one evening with friends. Died of a heart attack. I was in London when I got the call. Got into my car and drove nine hours straight to the Guynd. I was devastated. And then, to get here and find her gone. I guess I always thought she would be here. She always was."

Even if in Tom's opinion the Guynd would never give them any pleasure, or perhaps because he was so sure of it, Doreen was determined that it was the one thing they had that was worth her while to save. "I have to stay for the sake of the boys," she would explain to friends. "It's their heritage."

How were the boys to interpret this heritage, raised in the teeth-gritting cold passion of their parents conflicting dreams and desires? How was John to proceed under the heavy memory of a father who did not want him to inherit the family home, and a mother who sacrificed everything so that he could? Now the estate was in the hands of trustees his father had appointed, whose management over the years had been, at best, indifferent. Four hundred acres of farmland had been sold off to give Angus his share of the inheritance, which left John the sole beneficiary of what remained of a crippled and neglected estate—the land, the house, and its contents.

Was it the Guynd, I wondered, that engendered conflict, that raised hopes and guaranteed disappointment? Was it the Guynd that ruined Tom and Doreen's marriage? Angus and Alison's? No wonder John had held out for so long, observing these casualties with a cautious eye. Yet as outwardly critical as he was of the immediate precedents, did he really have the distance it would require to break the mold? No question about it. We were in a high-risk relationship.

IN NOVEMBER FRIENDS came over from Glasgow. Bar was an old childhood friend of mine from Boston who had married a Scot and moved to Glasgow some twenty years before me. Now fully indoctrinated in Scottish life, she was also very much the same hearty, ever optimistic person I had known as a child. She and her husband were both music people. Bar was a cellist. Her husband, John Purser, a musicologist and playwright, was also a walking encyclopedia of Scottish history and culture.

John and I had visited them the previous July in their crofter's cottage on the Isle of Skye. A spectacular spot, we were assured, though for two days that was entirely left to our imagination as we could hardly see more than five feet in front of us through the mist and driving rain. "Typical island weather," said my John, ever ready to extol the superior climate of Scotland's east coast. "It's much drier where we are." To which the other John replied, "Oh, but it's colder too," and on would go the Highlander-Lowlander one-upmanship that the Scots, I learned, can rarely resist.

The two Johns fished for crabs from an old wooden rowboat in the bay below the cottage at the bottom of the cliff. "Bloody freezing out there!" muttered one John, as he staggered into the cottage, dripping wet. (We Lowlanders live a more civilized life.) "Good for the circulation!" rejoined the other John. (We Highlanders are made of tougher stuff.) Later we picked the meat from the crabs, sitting around a fire of peat bricks that John and Bar had cut themselves from a bog nearby.

When the sky finally cleared we climbed a mountain, barefoot. "We don't bother with shoes, they'll only get soggy," explained Bar. She was right. The boggy hillside was wet but soft under our bare feet. From the top of the mountain as we watched the last of the mist evaporate and the late afternoon sun shone across the water, the hills in the distance changed from gray to dark blue. I felt as if I'd reached the end of the earth. "It all depends on your orientation," explained John Purser. "From my point of view we're very centrally located here, exactly halfway between Glasgow and the Outer Hebrides."

Clearly these people were not the type to be intimidated by the Guynd in late autumn, an unheated house, a bit of dust, or a lumpy sofa. Arriving one wet and windy November afternoon, Bar and John were impressed with the place at once and more than ready to pitch in to whatever task looked most pressing.

The news that we were engaged roused them to even greater enthusiasm. The house and grounds must be prepared for a great celebration. Setting out with gardening tools—Bar and I with what John called "lady's loppers" and the two Johns with heavier instruments for fatter branches—we cleared a path through overgrown rhododendrons around what was once an ornamental "loch." Back at the house over a cup of tea in the chilly drawing room I talked of our intention to raise more linoleum off the floors. Before John had even had a chance to consider how he might slow the momentum we were all on our feet, moving the grand piano and other large pieces of furniture around and heaving up great slabs of the stuff. We cleared the floor from the drawing room right through to the library. Then we all collapsed until dinnertime, while John frowned, feeling outnumbered, wondering if these new forces blowing through his old house were to be entirely trusted.

Bar and I improvised an Angus fish chowder with the local smoked peppered mackerel and potatoes out of our own fields. With oatcakes and salad and Stilton cheese and plenty of wine we ate and drank after a long day's work. After dark, around the dinner table with the shimmer of old silver and glass in the candlelight and the laughter of friends, I felt as far away and out of time as anyone could hope to be. We lingered, as people do here. There was no reason to hurry. Nothing happening here except us, nothing outside but the hoot of an owl or the flicker of a bat, while indoors we hovered on a classical cloud.

Washing up under the fluorescent light of the kitchen after dinner that night, John Purser took me aside in his authoritative and confidential manner and said, "You know of course what you have to do now, don't you, Belinda?"

"No, what?" I was longing to hear.

"You have to produce an heir!"

Little did any of us know at the time that an heir was already on his way.

FOUR

The Blessing

. . .

MY BREASTS FELT UNUSUALLY HARD AND ROUND AND sensitive. I was ravenous an hour after breakfast. I felt deeper than ever inexplicable wells of passion. I missed a period. "John, I think I'm pregnant," I announced one morning in early December.

Neither of us had ventured to discuss the possibility of having children together. We were too old to count on it. We had, I think, an unspoken understanding that discussing it would only make it less likely to happen. "Well you'd better get one of those home pregnancy tests and be sure," John advised, his practical side quickly following his initial shock.

It was as if somebody else had taken over the script, without even bothering to consult the main characters in the play. The story was getting ahead of us. We had so many improvements to make on the house and on the grounds. I was under contract with my publisher to finish my book. And by the way we weren't even married.

Back in New York in January we hastily tied the knot with a JP on the twelfth floor of One Center Street. Traveling downtown by subway from the Upper East Side, we stood in line for our turn at a booth, then sat in a waiting room on plastic chairs, surrounded by assorted, soon-to-be-legal aliens. My brother Peter left his office and met us there to be the only witness to the five-minute ceremony, if you could call it that.

I was either lucky or just too distracted to be sick. I spent the rest of the winter chasing up the last of my Walker Evans research, visiting archives and conducting interviews in New York and New Haven, and traveling as far as New Orleans and New Mexico, knowing that after the baby arrived I would be more or less housebound. John returned to the Guynd ahead of me to look after the next season of farm lets. In April, daffodil time, I returned to Scotland, six months pregnant with what we knew by then to be a boy.

John and Foxy met me at Heathrow and we headed north. It's a nine-hour drive from London to the Guynd, but it had become our habit to take at least three days to get there, stopping to visit cousins and view country houses along the way. This time we had planned a tour of houses designed, or "improved," by Robert Adam: Osterley Park in the outskirts of London, Kedleston in Derbyshire, Newby Hall and Nostell Priory in Yorkshire. What not so long ago I would have dismissed as overbearing architecture—unimaginable to live in with its elaborate plasterwork, gilded furniture, damask upholstery, and pompous

portraits—I now regarded as an ardent enthusiast. I was
ravenous for visual information, determined to get a better sense of the neoclassical country house—its strict symmetry, its harmony of color and proportion, its airy vistas.
Between visits, with John at the wheel, I pored over guidebooks and history books, spouting my newfound knowledge (a folly is not the same thing as a temple) and pepper-
ing John with questions (What's the difference between a
hectare and an acre? What are muniments?).

At the approach to Kedleston I admired a long avenue
of huge trees. "Lime, you call it linden in America," said
John. "Very typical. You can tell by the way the leaves
grow right to the base of the trunk." Inside the house I
noticed a wooden panel carved to look like folded cloth.
"That's called a linen fold pattern," John explained.

"Not made by the yard," I said, catching on now.

"I should say not."

While I admired such places as works of art, produced
for the sake of pleasure and enlightenment, John was more
inclined to regard them as simply work, somebody's work,
or the work of nature. Or the work of man and nature combined. Our exchanges consisted of my exclamations of
beauty, followed by his explanations of craft.

Never was there so much as a whisper of the families
who still lived in these great houses, now open to the public for what is Britain's largest tourist trade: the heritage
business. They were closed off in their private apartments,
of which behind the many interior doors there was no

hint, as tourists like ourselves quietly buzzed around, sizing up their pictures and furniture, strolling through their kitchen gardens and down avenues of shaped yews and woodland paths, having tea and scones in their converted stables, and finally packing off with National Trust coffee mugs and pot holders at the end of the day. Did they creep out to reclaim their grand rooms, to wander the halls or pull a book off the shelf in the library after the shop locked up and the guards went home?

I felt grateful for the luxury of our privacy. There were no tourists to hide from at the Guynd. Yet we too were about to be on view. We were expecting a small tribe of my relatives from America in August, for the double ceremony of the "blessing" of our marriage (as the minister had explained a wedding is called after the fact) and the christening of our child. What would our American guests think of Scotland in the first place, I wondered. It wasn't England, not at all. You notice the change as soon as you cross the border on the A68 just south of Jedburgh, something monochrome about the palette, something pared down about the buildings. "What is it that makes these towns so much more dour looking than the ones we've just traveled through?" I asked John.

"The eaves," he answered promptly. "The width of the eaves on the buildings. They're rather economical with them up here."

It's not long before you get used to a poverty of visual excitement in Scotland and train your eye instead to appreciate, say, the little cascade of matching chimney pots that descend down the typical small-town High Street. Or the way an old stone farmhouse is sited so snugly in the landscape, and the knowledge that many houses (like the Guynd) are completely hidden from the road, beyond the fields of wheat and barley and grazing animals, somewhere up that drive lined with wind-sculpted beech trees, out of sight.

Back at the Guynd the challenge before us was more vivid than ever. Faded and drab upholstery everywhere, a dulling coat of dust on every surface, no color, no shine. The place was starved of the brilliant hues and textures that made those other houses we had just visited so rich and beautiful. How, in a matter of weeks, were we to make the place look festive and welcoming? Grand but not pompous? Historically true without being a slavish attempt to re-create an impossible past? Most of all, I wanted it to be a warm, clean, and bright place to greet the first few months of our baby's life.

I had no choice but to become desperately interested in interior decoration. Shelter magazines stacked up beside the loo, where I found myself lingering over the back pages with the small ads for secondhand curtains, vintage bathroom fixtures, and radiator grilles. John had so far fulfilled his promise to paper our bedroom in an old-fashioned pattern of climbing roses I'd selected from the copious files of Colefax and Fowler, the company best known for traditional English country-style papers and fabrics. The pattern coincided perfectly with a vague fantasy I had long harbored of a bedroom in a country house. I replaced the gloomy landscapes over the fireplace with a new find from the cellar—two handsomely framed George Morland prints of pastoral youths lolling under oak trees and fishing from shady bridges. I moved a little armchair next to the fireplace, "a nursing chair," John informed me. The room was transformed. I woke up and felt happy.

If first impressions are the most important, however, it was now the front hall that was our most urgent project. Every time I entered the house it was a struggle to shake off the impression that I had entered a temple of gloom. The grubby yellow walls, the black columns, and the ceiling crisscrossed with thin strips of wood in a pattern of squares—at some stage a cheap attempt to affect the look of a coffered ceiling, as if it was possible to make the space feel smaller, or its claims more modest, or its style anything but Georgian.

Those country house visits were beginning to pay off. I was beginning to be able to articulate the problem. I was tossing around words like *architrave* and *entablature* with convincing ease. I could argue with some authority that everything the recent inhabitants had done to the hall vied to deny what it was designed to be—a grand welcome, a statement of taste and authority, a midway station between indoors and out, a place for the tenant, the salesman, the postman, or casual passerby to pause and chat, or for family and friends to shed their coats and boots before being shown through one of two pairs of laburnum-veneered doors to the left or right, into the inner sanctum.

THE HOUSE WAS designed two hundred years ago for John's namesake, John Ouchterlony, the same eighteenth-century gent whose Age of Reason smile beamed reassuringly over our heads from the portrait in the dining room. As he was the only son (with three older sisters) and heir to a promising estate, his family decided that he should graduate from the modest house by the *burn* (Scottish for stream) into something newer, bigger, and more fashionable. Farming was a booming business in late-eighteenth-century Britain; landowners found themselves suddenly rich with the agricultural improvements that by then had reached the wilds of Scotland. A country house architecture emerged to match their newfound prosperity—typically, a classical villa that presided over its open landscape with large windows and wide-open views and, in turn, an impressive-looking edifice as seen from a stroll around "the policies."

The original drawings by its architect, John Patterson of Edinburgh, were in a heap in the library. The title page announced in curvaceous eighteenth-century script, "A mansion house for John Ouchterlony Esq., of Guynd, 1799." These elevations and floor plans, rendered in deep black ink and tinted with aqua blues and porphyry pinks, were themselves seductive objects. To contemplate them in the late twentieth century, even with their crumbling edges suggesting decades spent in some damp corner of the house, was to share in the young squire's anticipation of a brand-new house, a new order in his life. From every angle the building was justified, with each room's specific function spelled out in expert calligraphy, "Front Hall," "Library," "Drawing Room," "Nursery." As the Ouchterlonys' plan grew more ambitious, a second set of drawings added two wings to the main facade, thus enabling the fashionable trend for an enfilade of rooms, one opening into the next, and into the next.

The plan was pure Regency—a blend of grand old Georgian combined with a rising trend of eclectic informality. Here the country squire could graciously entertain his family and friends and decorate to suit the function of each room. The dining room was the gentlemen's room, where they would linger after dinner with port and Stilton and cigars, take the ritual pee in a pot before joining the ladies who had "withdrawn" to the drawing room to discuss the latest servant problem or marital engagement. The library, a buffer zone between men and women after dinner, was the family room, in a time when books were the medium of informal congregation around the fire. Privacy was highly valued. Servants no longer stood at attention but disappeared up and down a network of hidden staircases at the back of the house.

In some respects, John Ouchterlony, Esq., was very much the man of his class and time. He traveled in Europe, painted landscapes in watercolor, wrote romantic poetry, and collected books as well as prints by Hogarth and Piranesi. He was an amateur in the days when that meant knowing a lot rather than knowing a little, as it does now. Like a growing number of landowners in those days, John

Ouchterlony spent part of the week in town, in his case the busy port of Montrose, about seventeen miles north of the Guynd, where he was involved in the shipping trade between Scotland and the Baltic. The Guynd was the family seat, and Ouchterlony's country residence where he could retreat for the pleasures of solitude and country pastimes.

Yet as the country squire John Ouchterlony did not altogether conform to the fashionable ideal. He never married, and perhaps it was due to his unmarried state that John Ouchterlony was, according to one local history, "far from careful in his dwelling, as he made no repairs, and it was rapidly becoming decayed." Apparently he also neglected the grounds, which upon his death "were all but tangled wild."

For John, this failure to conform only added to his ancestor's allure and mystery. His solitary nature, his eccentricity, his taste for art and literature were all a part of his appealing nature, a character who favored sensibility over sense. *He was an artist! He liked to read!* John would say in his ancestor's defense, implying somehow that a man who liked to read couldn't be expected to be good at managing an estate as well. Most of all, his reluctance to fulfill the role of laird as it was laid out for him struck an especially deep chord in my John. He claimed him—this fourth cousin four times removed—as his romantic legacy. But this was all the stuff of family legend or speculation. What proof did we have of his character, other than these historical fragments, other than his kind, wise face in the dining room portrait? What future did he hope for the Guynd after he was gone?

Ten years after his death his nephew John Alexander Pierson, to whom he had willed the entire estate, built a temple in his memory at the Guynd. John Ouchterlony had written his own elegy, and his words were carved into the stone walls of his memorial.

Though I'd heard of this temple, I had spent weeks at the Guynd the summer before without a clue as to how to get there. During my walks around the place it was nowhere in sight. Finally, at my urging, John led me up an inconspicuous path off the road about a mile from the house, through a grove of beechwood towering over us (was it Wordsworth who wrote of a *cathedral* of trees?), and high up a ravine overlooking the burn to where it stood. There in this concealed and secret place was a small neoclassical open air rotunda, as romantic as the ode John Ouchterlony wrote to his ancestors and to the landscape that would outlive them all. His words, carved into the inner stone wall of the temple, had been worn away by the elements. I fingered them like a blind woman reading Braille and managed to make out the words.

> *In this lone spot by mortal seldom trod*
> *The dust is laid, the spirit fled to God*
> *Of him, who reared these woods, these cultur'd plains*
> *With verdure cloth'd, or stor'd with golden grains*
> *O'er these paternal scenes by time defaced*
> *Bade yonder mansion rise in simple taste*

And deeming naught his own which heaven bestow'd
Diffused his blessings as a debt he ow'd.
Oh empty record! What avail thee now
Thy anxious days, thy labour warm'd brow.
See where man's little works himself survive
How short his life who bade these forests live,
While they shall rear their ample boughs on high
Through distant ages, and while o'er them sigh
Eve's murmuring breezes to the thoughtful say
Like his shall pass thy fleeting span away.

Those murmuring breezes had already begun to cast their spell on me; those ample boughs on high seemed to rise above everything prosaic and material. I was ready to receive the romantic wisdom of John's ancestors. For the Guynd was a continuum, an evolution, of which I now found myself a part. I was joining a succession of Guynd wives, each of us having entered a scene—at roughly fifty-year intervals—that was begging for total renewal.

IT WAS ELIZABETH PIERSON who first decorated the mansion house and brought it to life, while her husband, John Ouchterlony's nephew, James, made it "wind and water tight," and the landscape "into scenes of beauty." Just to be sure that her own family history would not be entirely overwhelmed by his—born a Grant of Glenmorriston, Elizabeth was the one who had descended from three kings—she had her own family's coat of arms incorporated into the cornice of the library. Some fifty years later John's grandmother Marie Wilmot endowed the Guynd with her family money, by which time it was badly needed to repair the roof and refurbish the kitchen. She opened the grounds to the public, and graced the town with her sense of charitable duty and devotion to the local Catholic church. John's mother brought her southern wit, her musical ear and her grand piano, her tennis racquet and golf clubs, and her strength of character during wartime.

What was I supposed to bring? What debt did I owe, and how to fulfill it in my own fleeting span? My predecessors were all British-born and therefore had the instinct and the training to run a country house. They would have known how to entertain, how to decorate, whom to call, what to say. They would have known how to talk to the gardener, the farmer, the gamekeeper, how to navigate the class system from top to bottom. Was I supposed to represent a break from this structured past, a breath of fresh air from overseas, a boldness of spirit perhaps that might once and for all admit that it was over? No matter what, I was in deep, way over my head.

For this was a house that demanded you to live up to it, to grow up to it, in a way that was more grown up than I had ever expected to be. I had no experience with rooms of these proportions or with architecture of this gravity. Small gestures were lost in the spaces, but large gestures were all the more daunting. Bringing in anything new and bright ran the risk of startling the old and making it look even more drab and sad than it already did.

Bearing down over all of these considerations was the postwar ethic deeply etched into the Ouchterlony psyche: to spend as little money as possible and to do most of the work themselves. Between the income from the farm and cottage rents, my barely respectable earnings as a writer, and some family investments on both sides, which could hardly bridge the gaps, we did indeed need to mind the bank balance. John was the policeman of waste and extravagance. Okay, I got my fancy floral wallpaper, let's not go crazy.

I ransacked the cellar, searching for clues as to how the rooms were once decorated. I heaved about piles of sun-bleached chintz fitted to sofas and chairs long since departed. 1920? I inspected curtains that might be worked into upholstery, some with patterns faded beyond recognition, others too heavy and Victorian for my taste. 1860? But then, my taste would have to change, to adapt to the climate and the locale. Out with the subtle grays, earth tones, and off-whites that might look cool and elegant in a city apartment. In with the rich and bold, the layered, the tasseled, the lustrous. As a start I had brought over a roll of fabric from a discount house in New York, a sturdy diamond pattern—red, green, and pale gold—that I thought would look just right in the library. I decided that the despised-looking Morris-type chair in the hall could be sacrificed to my first stab at amateur upholstery.

It turned out to be messy but not difficult work. There were no springs to fix; no curves, no stitching involved; it was just a matter of lifting the old fabric, keeping the stuffing under control, and tacking on the new, nice and tight. With a trim of gold braid glued and nailed around the edges, I concealed all my frayed edges and crooked tacks. I moved the great hulk into the library and placed it near the window, and it looked like a throne. "He actually let you do that?" asked Rita Adam, incredulous.

After that triumph I decided to tackle the fire stool, a long, low stool, a favorite of dozing dogs over the years, pockmarked here and there with charred black holes right through to the horsehair by errant sparks from the fire and more or less permanently draped with an even more dreadful-looking cloth that was meant to protect it. John pronounced my new upholstery "wildly impractical" and continued to throw a rag over it whenever we lit a fire.

Meanwhile, we pondered what color to paint the front hall. I invited Stephen up from the West flat to lend his artist's eye to the situation. Stephen said he liked it just the way it was, which didn't help. I myself was leaning cautiously toward a sort of grayish green. John came through with a strong vote for hot amber. He'd lived through enough Scottish winters. He knew too well how even summer had its fair share of cloudy days. Irresistibly drawn to warm colors, he was downright intolerant of cool ones. In the end, John's certainty won out.

The columns had to be considered at the same time. Should they be lighter or darker than the walls? Receding or dominant? Marbled or plain? I returned to my books on old houses, and I thought of Kedleston, Syon House, Osterley. Deciding on a white/gray marbling effect, I also managed with some difficulty to dissuade John from a self-taught crash course in faux painting, and we found a young couple from Edinburgh who were just getting their start in the business, eager for the work, and could be hired cheap. John was thus released to get on with the less appealing tasks, stripping the brown paint off the skirting and door surrounds and untacking the strips of wood from the ceiling.

Armed with a dozen or so wallpaper samples I had ordered up from London and paint swatches from the nearest DIY emporium, I tried with difficulty to envision a total transformation. When we tested the amber on the wall it shocked, but nicely. A few more strokes of the roller and Mediterranean sunshine nudged aside Scottish gloom. We erected the scaffolding, bought and stirred the paint. Now the only problem was to get on with it.

I thought we had an understanding. Wasn't the hall our number one project now? But I was beginning to realize that while my point of pride was the look of the interior of the house, John's was the exterior. His mind was preoccupied with fixing the lawn mower, which had "packed up" (broken down) for about the third time that summer. While waiting for a spare part to come into the mechanic's shop in Dundee the grass was becoming ragged, the clover was starting to sprout. "If you let the lawn go, that's it," said John.

The closer we came to embarking on the painting of the hall, the further away it seemed to stretch. The more I pressed John, the more he would stall, express some other

priority, and remind me that, after all, we hadn't even finished the preparation—the cleaning, the spackling, the
sanding. "It's ninety percent of the job!" he would say,
which left him holding all the cards. For there was no way
my preparation could live up to the exacting standards of
the engineer. It was June. The baby was due in a month.
But John kept disappearing, apparently finding more
important things to do "out in the back." I would find him
in the garage, his long face bent over a pile of tools, sorting, glasses perched at the end of his nose, deep in his
work. "That's an indoor job," he'd say about the hall.
"Wait for a rainy day, there's too much else to do." There
was this plan if it rained, and that plan if it didn't, while the
Scottish sky hung typically in gray, mysterious silence,
giving away nothing but an occasional tantalizing flash of
sunshine. John was teasing me. He was deliberately testing my patience, reminding me of the countless tasks
involved in keeping up the place, and exactly where decorating stood in the overall scheme of things. To worry
about it too much was bourgeois, really, pretentious, even.

"Was your mother *pretentious*, then," I challenged
him, "with her curtains and slipcovers? Was it *pretentious*
of her to care how this house looked? How she might
make her guests feel comfortable and as if she might be
expecting them?"

No answer.

I was beginning to suspect that John actually preferred to have the place in a state of process, with scaffolding and tools everywhere, as if to make sure that every-

one—especially our guests—could see for themselves
that he was in the midst of his work and that his work had
no end. While John carried in his head a long list of projects he felt were priorities, I was rapidly forming a list of
my own. While he was working on a grand plan with no
time limit, a scheme of so many parts that he had written
and rewritten in his mind over the years, I had no access to
it. Immediate deadlines seemed to have no impact on his
thinking. Things would happen "in due course."

Just to add another complication to our lives, Foxy
came "into season," as they delicately put it here, and we
had decided to breed her at the next opportunity, as she
was already eight years old, to extend her excellent character to the next generation. We also felt that as she had
been our only child, she might feel jealous of the new
arrival. With offspring of her own, we figured, she would
be too distracted to worry about ours. We set her up with
a pure-bred Vizla, a Hungarian pointer of elegant
physique John had met at the pet shop in Dundee. A
bounding young brown dog by the name of Rusty arrived
on a lead with his master, and Foxy, after a half hour of
flirtation—chasing around the place, a good deal of sniff-
ing and vigorous wagging of tails—finally got young
Rusty down to business. We expected puppies in early
August.

A week away from delivering our own, I was high up
on the scaffolding in the hall, paintbrush in hand, picking
out the egg-and-dart pattern of the cornice in yellow and
white, while BBC Radio Four mumbled continuously in

the background: the mysterious poetry of the shipping forecast (Tyree eight, winds southwest five, eight miles, falling) or the cozy chatter of the "Gardener's Question Hour" (How do you keep the flea moths off the peas without using chemicals? Answer: a fine mesh. Which plants will help to keep the riverbank from eroding? Periwinkle, Autumn Joy, marsh marigolds, skunk cabbage) or "The World at One" with occasional news from home (record-high temperatures and low rainfall in the western United States have allowed for rampant forest fires). Then suddenly one evening, earlier than expected, my water broke and we rushed off to the hospital in Dundee. After twenty hours of labor, with the help of an Icelandic obstetrician, two midwives, and John, I delivered our baby boy.

We had decided to name him John, but to call him by his middle name, Elliot, after the burn, the "Elliot Water," that runs through the Guynd. Moved by the words of his ancestor's poem we wanted to honor the landscape that would outlive us all. And like a river, Elliot knew exactly what to do, even if I didn't. To breathe, to suck, to sleep. This baby had an authority and a confidence in me that was like a pact between us he'd already written in the womb. Having carried him for nine months I suddenly realized when I met him face to face that we had hatched a person with a character and a destiny all his own. John noticed the strength of his grip on his finger. I noticed the power of his tug at my breast. And we both noticed to our surprise, though there was very little of it, that his hair was red.

Back from the hospital with the infant Elliot, in the haze of the mystery of the child who had suddenly arrived to take over our lives, and the energy I was calling up from depths I never knew were there, we resurrected the old crib from the cellar, a "Moses" basket from the old cook's room, moth-eaten blankets and hand-knit sweaters from dresser drawers, embroidered bibs from the linen cupboard. Bundled for warmth, Elliot toured the house on my shoulder, by day staring wide-eyed at the sunshine through the cupola and, in the evening, at the light from the dancing fire.

My mother flew over to help, to counsel, and to comfort. She immediately saw, as mothers will, how much support I needed with both child care and housekeeping, and how John might be slower than she to recognize these newfound challenges. We discovered that Carol, a cheerful blond middle-aged woman who with her husband, Erwin, had moved into one of the farm cottages, was happy to babysit a few hours a day. With grown children of her own, Carol was a natural; she was happy to return to the fond memories of her own young motherhood. "Righty-ho then!" she'd say to me, taking Elliot into her experienced arms, "you go have yourself a break."

An old family friend in the village recommended her neighbor Kathy to clean the house. Strong, tall Kathy arrived to view the job, was interested in the house, and, best of all, not put off by a task I was presently to learn no other would ever dare to take on. Although John was not sure that anyone could be trusted to clean the house prop-

erly, nor whether it was necessary to spend the ten quid it
would cost us to find out, Kathy was not intimidated by
his quiet air of doubt, nor by the antique equipment he
offered her to work with. She dodged that issue by packing her own Electrolux and quickly figured out how to zip
through the house (at least the parts we moved through
daily) in three hours flat. At the end of each session she
declared optimistically, "We're getting there!"

One day my mother and I attacked the old cloak room
and amassed piles of ragged, stained, and rotten old jackets and shoes and boots for the trash. Then John opened
up the wheelybins in the back and found his hobnailed
boots and his boiler suit in the mix and my mother experienced the first sting of his disapproval, although I was the
one who took the heat.

A cold war between the sexes ensued with my mother
and I and Elliot snubbing John for dinner that night. Later
my mother took John aside and told him squarely, "I have
to warn you that even if your mother was a saint, you can
be sure that Belinda is not!" (I was eventually to determine
that Doreen was not a saint either, in spite of all the praying. Like a lot of wives, she didn't confront the opposition
as much as figured out how to work behind his back.)

Truces were made by the next morning for there was
no time to lose. Suddenly the house was buzzing with
activity. My mother found Doreen's old sewing box and
got busy mending clothes, replacing missing buttons,
darning socks. John set up a worktable with paste and
Exacto knife and hung new wallpaper in the library—a

dense burnt-orange floral motif flecked with gold that echoed the gold leaf of the old book bindings and looked at once as if it had always been there. For several days the faux painters balanced on ladders around the columns in the front hall with their brushes and feathers, oils and paints. Meanwhile Foxy and I nursed our babies. Regarding with delighted astonishment his wife and his dog in our new roles, John now referred to us collectively as "the mothers." He referred to Elliot as "the sprout" and, as much as he admired him, was more apt to be found cuddling the puppies.

I scoured old books in the library for whimsical motifs for the birth announcement and invitations to the blessing, while John tried to remember who he knew in Angus and if they were still there. Childhood friends, old friends of his parents, neighboring farmers, and longtime tenants formed the core of our list. We remembered my cousins in Hampshire and Oxford, John's in London and Sussex, and from America my parents, brother and sister, their children, and the godparents whose support we summoned to christen Elliot at the temple.

The service had to be planned, caterers found, accommodations for guests arranged, music for both ceremony and dancing. We called up an Episcopal minister from London to perform the blessing and christening, John's relation by marriage, the Reverend John Salter, who accepted with enthusiasm.

Mrs. Sheret, an old lady in the village who used to cook for John's mother, offered to make the wedding cake.

As the Guynd cook, Mrs. Sheret was famous for starting the brussels sprouts at ten o'clock for lunch at one. But one didn't argue with the help, which was hard to get, especially one who so admired the lady ("Mrs. Ouchterlony was such a lady," she told me every time we met) and who shared her passion for needlework. I carefully provided Mrs. Sheret with her list of ingredients for the traditional dark, dense fruit cake, topped with a thick layer of marzipan and encased in a sheet of white icing sugar, smooth as porcelain. I arrived at her cottage with icing sugar, almond paste, dried fruit, and she showed me the little cones she made out of paper with which to squeeze out the intricate iced decorations.

Bar and John called up a flutist for the procession and a band for dancing Scottish reels at the reception. An artist from Arbroath offered to make bouquets for my four nieces as flower girls to carry at the blessing. John cleared the path to the temple and replaced the bridges over the Elliot Water with old wooden farm pallets so that our little christening party, young and old, could make the half mile trek safely through the woods and up the ravine to the sacred spot.

By the time we opened our doors for the festivities in late August, the scaffolding was dismantled, the pillars were convincingly marbled, the hall was gloriously golden-yellow. I had rearranged various pieces of furniture and hidden others, switched some curtains around, cleared quantities of furniture and bric-a-brac away. I had resurrected several Piranesi prints from the cellar and hung two of them in the hall. The lawn looked almost as smooth as a golf course, and pots of bright geraniums decorated the front steps. The Guynd was beginning to smile, as Alison would say. But would our guests have any idea how much we had done, when what was more obvious was how much there was yet to do?

The three-day party washed over me like a dream. The machinery we had put in place took over and our guests from near and far seemed to know exactly what to do. Victoria, Elliot's American godmother, took my four nieces on a wildflower expedition, returned with armloads of daisies, goldenrod, and Queen Anne's lace, arranged them in vases, and dotted them all over the house. When the heavens opened on our blessing on the lawn and rain fell, our guests popped open their umbrellas, my nieces, clutching their bouquets, stood their ground bravely, my sister Eliza tucked baby Elliot under her raincoat, and the minister carried on with our solemn vows as raindrops wet through the thin pages of his prayer book.

Back inside the house everyone mixed—Americans and Scots, farmers and gentry, old and young. The band members installed themselves under the staircase, and on the stone floor of the hall we danced Scottish jigs and reels, while children rushed in and out of the front door with handfuls of cereal to offer the puppies in the kennel. The dining room was laid with a cold buffet and more than enough pink Australian champagne. At the great moment when we called everyone into the dining room for the obligatory toasts, Mrs. Sheret's porcelain-smooth wedding cake resisted us like sheer ice, finally giving way under the pressure of our sharpest kitchen knife to jagged pieces. But nobody seemed to mind as we doled out helpings of massacred fruit cake onto a flurry of little plates, which my nieces cheerfully disbursed among our guests as Mrs. Sheret herself sat in a chair in the middle of the traffic, beaming with pride.

"Terribly clever of her to have produced an heir so quickly, don't you think?" I overheard Alison chatting to another guest.

"I *love* the color you painted the hall," an old friend of Doreen's said to me. "It's so daring!"

"Wonderful to see this old house filled with life again," said a neighboring farmer. "You don't like seeing a grand old place like the Guynd running down."

What they were saying among themselves I could only imagine. Fancy John with an American wife! I'm told she's literary. But does she know anything about running a farm?

I suddenly remembered to check on Elliot, whose little cries would not have been audible over the music and revelry. I was grateful for the excuse to step back from the party, as I nursed him, sitting unnoticed high up on the staircase with a bird's-eye view of our guests dancing below. Spying on the grown-ups, like the child I once was. But instead of the scent of perfume and smoke and the swell of conversation and laughter rising up the staircase as my parents and their guests approached the front door to depart for an art opening in town, here was the music of the Scottish Highlands, the exotic whine of the fiddle and squeeze box. As our guests formed squares of four couples for the traditional "Eightsome Reel," I marveled at how here, of all places, I had found myself the center of attention.

The next day a brisk wind blew the rain clouds away and the sun shone for the procession to Elliot's christening at the temple. Single file, we trekked through the woods to that "lone spot by mortal seldom trod." Elliot was doused with water fresh from the *burn* of his own name, as the Reverend Salter in his golden robes reminded the assembled that Elliot's ancestors had inhabited this countryside for at least eight hundred years.

As the dust settled again over the house, I wondered what impression the place had made on those who had come from so far away. My guess was that whatever envy they may have felt for the sheer romance of it all was well tempered with awe at the overwhelming task we faced. I asked my father if the Guynd was anything like what he had expected it to be. At eighty-three he was slowing down, but with effort on his part and patience on mine he could speak like the eloquent man he had always been. He had spent a lifetime of connoisseurship, visiting houses and collections all over the world, handling treasures of the centuries with taste and knowledge. How rich a memory bank he had to call upon, how many associations! He thought a long time, in his considerate way perhaps canceling out some of the less complimentary answers to my question, and finally said in summary, "I wasn't prepared for the height of the ceilings."

With Elliot the house took on an entirely new meaning. Did this tiny pilot on my shoulder, his eyes still glazed with early infancy, know the difference between indoors and out, as I carried him up the stairs or through the towering woods? At the Guynd, through his eyes, they seemed to me to be the same. "Before he is cast into the world,'" wrote Gaston Bachelard, "man is laid in the cradle of the house. And always, in our daydreams, the house is a large cradle." A very large cradle, in Elliot's case. And now that it was Elliot's cradle, it was also, suddenly, my home.

Part Two

FIVE

The Garden

. . .

THE FIRST TIME I ENTERED THE GARDEN I DIDN'T even know that I had.

I was walking with Foxy one morning when, about a quarter of a mile down the road from the house, I happened to notice a stone step just off to the right, under the trees. A pair of yews arched drunkenly over the step, like a clue in a long-forgotten gateway to something that once was. Wild foxgloves swayed their pink and white petals invitingly. Foxy, nose to the ground, led me through the yews at a trot, clearly as familiar with this piece of the territory as any other. My eyes adjusted to the sudden darkness. I found myself in a cave of laurel and rhododendron.

Before me was a little stone shed, missing its door, its slate roof covered in moss, on either side of it groves of whispering bamboo. Inside the shed the walls were lined from top to bottom with a geometric pattern of rough-hewn wood, with matching benches built into the length of each side. Straight ahead was an arched wrought-iron gate just my height. With a little shove I opened the gate against the will of the weeds on the other side, only to find myself up to my eyes in stinging nettle. Beyond that, all I could see was a gloomy thicket of pine woods. I retreated, calling Foxy. Though her head was already down a hole in the ground, her tail wagging vigorously, I knew of other, far brighter routes we could take.

So I continued to be puzzled when from time to time John mentioned "the garden," as if it were a place that still existed, which I might have seen. It was some time later when I realized that I had actually been there, that the little shed in the woods was the garden gate, and the thicket of pines was a Christmas tree farm John's father had planted back in the 1960s. The fourteen-foot stone wall around the garden, which John had spoken of with such emphasis, was too high and spread too far, too over-whelmed with vines and overshadowed by trees for me to have noticed it, from within or from without. For there was no within or without anymore. (As the Red Queen said to Alice, "I've seen gardens compared to which this is a wilderness!")

The next time I ventured into the garden, I armed myself with a "swiper," a long-handled instrument with a sharp-edged hook at the end, good for cutting away nettle or any other weeds in one's path. John's mother never took a walk without it, and John had several times suggested that I follow her example. Now inside the garden again, swiping away the nettle all around me, I began to discern the basic shape of the garden's one square acre. The stone wall surrounded it on just three sides, highest at the upper end, almost imperceptibly shortened as it followed the slope down to the terrace at the bottom and disappeared. The wall itself was scattered with little nails and the mossy skeletal remains of fruit trees were still frozen in espaliered contortions against it. Venturing into the center of the garden I encountered the ragged form of two parallel yew hedges, which once defined an open avenue. At the top of the garden a greenhouse, much of its glass shattered by falling limbs of Norway spruce, lined the center of the upper wall. Straight across the garden from where I had entered was another opening in the wall, sealed by a green door.

Beyond that door stood the original Guynd house, built circa 1615; this was the house where four generations of Ouchterlonys had lived and died. After the mansion house was built the original house was enlarged and remodeled as a dower house in the fashionable Victorian style of the cottage orné. Eventually it became the residence of the gardener, Mr. Prescott. But that was fifty years ago. Now it was derelict, with ivy nudging into its upstairs windows, slates missing from the roof, rotting floors, missing doors.

The stonemason's work may last for centuries, but the gardener's work is never done. As anyone with the smallest patch of a garden knows, it takes shockingly little time for nature to take charge once the gardener lets go. Ours was not the only kitchen garden of its size to have been abandoned in utter despair some time ago. English literature at the turn of the century abounds with oversize country houses—their aging owners huddled in the west wing, while the rest of the pile succumbs to dry rot—and every one of them has a kitchen garden, gone to seed. The abandoned kitchen garden has served as a symbol of old world values in hopeless decline, or, as I dimly recalled from reading *The Secret Garden* at age ten or eleven, a chance for renewal, when the spoiled and lonely Mary Lennox discovers friendship and compassion in her efforts to restore the abandoned garden of Misselthwaite Manor. But of all the dereliction country houses have suffered, the odds against resurrecting the garden are the greatest.

Taken in its prime, the garden at the Guynd is a textbook example of the typical kitchen garden of this part of the world. In every respect it is a model of logic, practicality, and beauty that has defined garden design since the seventeenth century when it was first laid out. It faces southwest to capture the warmest sunshine. Its gentle slope makes the most of the sun as well as encouraging the frost to roll off. The three-sided stone wall, open at the lower end and finished with a retaining wall, created a microclimate several degrees warmer than the land surrounding it. This also meant that its growing season was lengthened by several weeks at both ends, and its horticultural repertoire expanded to include all kinds of fruits and vegetables that would otherwise not survive so far north.

"I would advise you," wrote Mrs. Loudon, in *Lady's Country Companion* of 1845, which I pulled out of our library, "to have [the garden] surrounded by a wall about ten feet high for fruit trees." Loudon also advised that "the whole of the garden should be well drained, and you should contrive it so as to have easy access to either pond or river water." True to the book, a few steep yards beyond the terrace of the Guynd garden was the essential source of irrigation, the Elliot Water.

Unrolling an 1839 topographical survey of the Guynd estate, I could easily make out the little piece of geometry that was once the working kitchen garden. It shows that its layout was conventional, with straight intersecting paths dividing it into quarters. Vegetables planted in straight rows within the four oblong compartments might have included artichokes, rhubarb, horseradish, and asparagus—typical perennial crops in the Scottish kitchen garden. Onions, brussels sprouts, beetroot, all kinds of beans, lettuce, spinach, and potatoes named after noble breeders like King Edward and the Duke of York were planted each year. The gravel paths between the quarters were well drained and meticulously free of weeds; this was the thoroughfare of the gardener and his barrow. The crops were enclosed in low box edging to keep the earth from spilling out, and the gravel from spilling in.

Apple, peach, and pear trees were espaliered along the walls, catching the best of the sunshine and adding a decorative effect. In the greenhouse, or "forcing garden," tomatoes, cucumber, and melons got a head start on the season, with solar power enhanced by the heat of a coal stove.

In Scotland, I learned, it was typical to have a "mixed" garden, that is, to grow flowers and vegetables in the same enclosure. The English landscape gardener Charles Smith observed with apparent disdain that, in Scotland, "we not infrequently meet with extensive parks in which there is no separate flower garden, and where all the departments of both horticulture and floriculture are jumbled together in much confusion." Such was the case at the Guynd, at least by the turn of the century when John's grandparents added the decorative floral features then in fashion. The avenue of yews was clipped into fanciful topiary. A wide herbaceous border of delphinium, lobelia, salvia, larkspur, and hollyhock decorated the avenue between the yews. Old-fashioned climbing roses and clematis adorned the trellises that arched at intervals over the gravel path and led the eye to the vanishing point: the garden gate.

All year-round the household reaped the benefits of the garden. There were fresh fruits and vegetables for the table in the summer, flowers—fresh cut or dried—to decorate the hall, lavender in sachets to keep the dresser drawers smelling fresh, jars upon jars of pickled vegetables, vinegar, jams, and jellies in the kitchen cupboard, cider and wine in the cellar.

In John's grandparents' day it took two gardeners and "a boy" to keep the plants thriving and the weeds at bay. Even then there was concern about the creeping demise of large private gardens, the weaning away of gardening staff to industry and to the cities, and the need to plan gardens requiring less maintenance and reduced manpower. John's grandparents adopted the current fashion for the "wild" or "alpine" garden. Between the lower terrace and the *burn* they planted exotic new world species from western China, South America, and the American northwest: bamboo and rhododendron, Oriental maples and giant sequoia. Scottish horticulturists were known to be among the world's most voracious collectors of plants, perhaps because so many adapted well to Scotland's moist atmosphere. But by now the "wild" garden was truly wild, as if the exotic plants had been returned to the untamed new world jungles and forests from which they came.

The Guynd garden's demise was gradual, infinitesimal at first. Even after John's grandmother died in 1913 it continued to prosper under the care of Mr. Prescott, the head gardener, who still resided in the old house on the other side of the garden door. When the Coxes moved into the Guynd in 1930 it was still in respectable condition. Even John has a distant, subliminal memory of the garden in its prime, from the year he and his mother spent sheltered with the Coxes at the Guynd during the war. It's the kind of memory one has as a three-year-old—acutely sensual, visually fuzzy. He yearns for that Mediterranean whiff of boxwood and bay leaf, for the dry heat emanating from sunbaked stone walls, for the bright light unfiltered by trees. By the time the family moved back to the Guynd after the war, however, the garden had become weedy and disheveled. Mr. Prescott had died. The old house stood uninhabited.

Like many other landowners with gardens in a similar

postwar state and without a full-time gardener, John's father abandoned all hope of it ever being restored to its former glory. Growing flowers on anything but a modest scale was generally discouraged in those economically stressed times. At first, in favor of a more profitable plan, he offered it up as a market garden, in much the same way as he let the fields to agriculture. The idea was that the gardener paid rent for the garden, then sold whatever he grew to a local market. But the Guynd's market gardener, like so many others in the region, did not find it economically viable, and eventually he let the garden go. In the 1960s there was a growing trend for turning old gardens into Christmas tree plantations. John's father tried this also, but the tree business was unsuccessful as well, partly due to the emerging vogue for artificial Christmas trees. By the time failure dawned he could not be bothered to harvest the trees, most of which were already too big to get into the average cottage living room, let alone through the garden gate.

WHAT SHOULD WE DO?

An abandoned garden's demise would be less painful, it could have been altogether forgotten, if it weren't for the wall reminding us of its structure, of its prominence once upon a time. It was still a place, really an extension of the original Guynd house, and at one time just as important. Furthermore, the wall was worth saving and, with it, the site was a warm sheltered spot in the landscape, ideal for growing things.

I myself have no gardening talent whatsoever. Making decisions about what to plant in the assorted pots on the front steps, or what to fill in that blank spot of ground next to the azalea, had already challenged the limits of my daring. At the garden center I would stare blankly at the hollyhocks, asking myself if they were too tall, or were the white marguerites too plain, or the lady's mantle too invasive, and finally walk away, empty-handed, in a haze of confusion and self-doubt. In wonder and delight I look upon the bold strokes of the master gardeners who know how to orchestrate the growing season, how to layer and sequence the colors and textures so that they seem to burst forth in harmonious song of their own accord, hiding the decay the past performance as they protect the birth of the new all summer long.

Touring our friends' garden at nearby Dunninald Castle, I imagined how the Guynd garden used to be. The perfectly pruned fruit trees trained to the wall, the arches over the gravel paths bedecked with climbing roses, the diciplined rows of vegetables—bulb artichokes as high as your head, beefy cabbages, runner beans trained to their climbing frame—made just as good a show as the herbacious border, a blowsy spray of lobelia and larkspur. This mixed garden was anything but confusing.

"How did this garden survive so well over the years? Did it ever get out of control?" I asked Rosalinde, the lady of the house, whose devotion and good taste made this the most beautifully preserved garden in the county.

"We were fortunate," she answered. "Dunninald wasn't requisitioned during the war. It was a little too remote. So it was saved."

"It's very Scottish, isn't it," I ventured, testing the validity of my background reading, "to have the vegetables and the flowers in the same enclosure?"

"Yes, I suppose it is," answered Rosalinde, never having thought about it that way, I supposed; it was just the way it was. "Aren't you clever!"

Well, hardly as clever as she was. If I had a gardening instinct at all it was not so much to grow things as to prune and shape or, in a more drastic frame of mind, to turf up that distorted piece of shrubbery altogether.

Back at the Guynd I discovered that the boxwood tree behind the drying green that was meant to be in the shape of a giant ball was wonderfully responsive to shears. It cut easily and wiggled back into form like a perfectly coiffed head of hair. The holly tree on the side of the lawn was an altogether different kind of customer. It was prickly, for one thing, and working close to its rangy branches I found it difficult to keep track of my progress. Old Will Crighton looked on in dismay as I wobbled, loppers in hand, at the top of a ladder.

"Do ya ken [know] it takes twa [two] people to prune a holly," he explained, "one up the ladder, the other on the ground telling him where to cut."

No one had ever told me that, no. Furthermore, Crighton added with a sigh, "That's a winter job, that is."

Obviously. When the tree stops growing. I was fighting a losing battle with nature. And another thing, "With a wind like this you canna see what you're doing."

I really hadn't thought this through.

"And how's the wee *bairn* [Scottish baby, child]?"

Better I should just carry on with motherhood, I think he meant.

John, on the other hand, possesses the opposite instinct from mine, that is, not to cut back at all but to grow things. He objected to my use of the word *dirt*. It sounded degrading. The word is *soil*. The sight of a seed—a beechnut or an acorn—incites his urge to propagate. A little row of pots along the edge of the old swimming pool that sprouted various species, which I kept forgetting to water, attested to this instinct. Yet in spite of his propensity for growing trees rather than cutting them down, John did feel that the garden was a special case. His childhood memory of the garden's delicious warmth and smell and his youthful anger at his father for giving it up to Christmas trees combined to haunt him. His instinct to preserve and to resurrect what was good about the past— nay, better—made him determined to set things right again. Though we had admitted it would be impossible to achieve a garden of real splendor again, just to cover it with rhubarb, artichokes, or asparagus, or some such easy-care crop, would be enough of an ambition. Or simply to mow it, or turn it into a sheep meadow rather than a forest. Anything to turn night back into day.

But how to remove the Christmas trees? Cut them

down, take them out? Unfortunately it's not as simple as that. How to move a fifty-foot tree through a six-foot garden gate? Or, having done that with some difficulty, what to do about the stumps? Grubbing them up would take a bulldozer, a machine we didn't own, and even if we did it could not fit through the gates.

With his engineering mentality John sees everything in terms of energy efficiency, both human and mechanical. He is sure that even in an imperfect world, full of imperfect people, there is a perfect solution. Having mulled over the problem for many years, he had become attached to a plan to pull the trees over—as the roots of pine trees are not too deeply embedded in the ground—thereby uprooting the stumps in the same gesture. But we were still faced with the constraints of working within the wall. Would the winch, needed to pull the trees over, be compatible with the crawler tractor John was planning to resurrect out of the farm buildings? One thing was certain. We weren't going to get anywhere without help.

The spring before Elliot turned three years old we came across a curious ad in *Historic House* magazine. It said, "Wanted: a kitchen garden about one acre in size," signed, "Robert Milne, organic gardener, Bucknell, Shropshire."

"Shropshire," said Elliot, savoring this new mouthful of a word.

"Shall we drop him a line?" I suggested to John.

Fully expecting this stranger to be put off by the news that our kitchen garden was way up north and full of

Christmas trees, I composed a letter (I was the composer of letters), and John approved it. Astonishingly, in spite of having had several other responses to his ad, Milne chose to pursue our garden. "I love creating order out of chaos," he wrote to us reassuringly. Even after traveling up to see it in all its stark reality Milne could not be put off. For though the prospect looked a bit daunting, he had the freedom and foresight to see it in the long term, and furthermore we were open to his plan, having not fully formed one of our own. The idea was that he would clean up the turf and establish it as a teaching garden. Ultimately, if all went well, he would move up to Scotland and use the garden to run courses and weekend workshops. All we had to do as a first step was pay him a modest salary and put him up for a few weeks over the summer, along with whatever volunteer help he could attract. He even suggested that we open the garden to visitors in its present state, as a sort of dare-the-impossible exhibit.

To meet him was to see that Milne was a man of his word. Slight and bearded, with his loose-cut gardening trousers and straw hat, he seemed to have hardly brushed with the twentieth century. It was impossible to discern the merest crack in his life ethic. He had a total disregard for power tools of any kind. All he asked of us, other than a stack of bread tins and a few pounds of organic flour, was the use of a scythe and a sharp ax. For he himself was the machine, going about his work rhythmically, methodically, scything away at the weeds, axing off the lower dead limbs of the spruce so that, little by little, light filtered into the garden. Occasionally he would come across an old root and inspect it, as a picture restorer might inspect the brushstroke of a Leonardo, and identify it as some kind of ancient pear tree. *Pyrus salicifolia!* He fueled himself on modest helpings of organic vegetables and homemade bread, and was politely appalled at the quantity and variety of our own food and drink. He disapproved of imported food of any kind. Australian cheddar? How could they justify the use of all that jet-engine fuel to import something we English make perfectly well ourselves?

Meanwhile three organic-minded students from St. Andrews composed a lighthearted team of volunteers, ready to camp out and eat homemade bread and lentils for the privilege of restoring a historic garden and hanging out with Robert Milne, organic guru, whom John by now simply called "the Tree," though not to his face. The sheer enormity of the endeavor made the students laugh when they first saw it. A thin solitary vegan also appeared, with his thin, loping dog named Free, to take up the challenge of stone wall repair. John put him to work reconstructing a corner of the lower terrace wall. I pulled together all I could find of a few black-and-white snapshots of the garden back in the 1930s in an effort to convince them (and myself as well) that, if it ever was, it could be again.

To prepare the ground for the tree-pulling operation, a few stray sycamores had to be felled and cleared. These, John admitted, could not be pulled out by the roots. It seemed that there was always the first problem to tackle before we could get to the main task. Now John appeared to be the late-twentieth-century man of progress, with his noisy electric chain saw that needed sharpening or tuning or filling up again with fuel, or some such delay, just when we thought we were getting somewhere, while Milne and his team quietly cut and stacked piles of brush and set them on fire. Next, John spent the better part of a week repairing an ancient crawler tractor, just small enough to fit through the garden gates, just big enough, he hoped, to pull over a tree.

By mid-August the stage was finally set to try out John's plan, and our manpower, having run out of time, had disappeared. Milne had symbolically planted a little row of broccoli in a bright patch of ground, but for all his steadiness and optimism he had not achieved a miracle. Still, we had addressed the garden instead of turning our backs on it. We had cleared enough dead wood to have a better grasp of its shape. We could now walk straight across it or straight down it through the wild garden to the *burn*. It was once again a focal point of an afternoon walk. We still had a long way to go.

WE SPENT OUR first Christmas at the Guynd that year. Elliot, aged three, was just old enough to feel the magic of Christmastime, to imagine Santa Claus flying overhead and dropping down the chimney to stuff his stocking to overflowing, and to thrill at the sight of a great Christmas tree.

I had been duly warned that Scotland was not famous

for its Christmas spirit. In the sixteenth century, when Scottish Presbyterianism was at its most aggressive, a man could be punished for not working on Christmas Day. As the Presbyterians softened the rules over the centuries, Christmas was acknowledged but hardly celebrated. A child could expect to be grateful for a halfpenny or, if he was especially lucky, a Seville orange, and that was about the end of it. The ritual of the tree, which Queen Victoria introduced to England in the 1870s, took almost a hundred years more to catch on in Presbyterian Scotland, at just about the time John's father planted out the garden with his crop of Norway spruce. Even so, John's mother was perpetually disappointed in the general lack of holiday spirit compared to that of her native England. She did her best to make up for it by decking the halls with boughs of holly, and there was plenty to gather from the overgrown holly trees right around the house. In her day branches of shiny dark green leaves and bright red berries sprouted jauntily from the tops of picture frames, ropes of ivy wound up the banister, Christmas cards strung on yarn hung in swags from the mantelpiece and bookshelves, until she could reasonably claim to have made the house jolly. But everywhere else she turned, in town or countryside, the holiday seemed all but forgotten. No Christmas lights brightened the streets of Arbroath, hardly a wreath decorated a door. As old Will Crighton put it, Christmas was just "anether dee."

For the Scots are deeply resistant to the possibility that any holiday might overshadow the far more important celebrations of Hogmanay (Hog-ma-*nay*), which is New Year's Eve. This is traditionally an all-nighter consisting of walking around the village with a bottle of not-the-best whisky in your pocket soon after the midnight hour has struck, never before. On the first stop you make, you must endeavor to send a dark-haired member of your party across the threshold first for good luck, and he or she should be carrying a lump of coal. Once inside, you offer your neighbors a wee dram of your bottle while they meantime insist that you imbibe in a wee dram of theirs. This is called the "first footing." The next stop is the second footing—though you don't have to worry about the dark-haired person anymore—and so on as long as you like, or are able, to stay on your feet. Don't ever try mixing this ritual with champagne.

I never really knew what "Auld Lang Syne" meant. Now I know that *auld* means old, and *lang* means long. *Syne* is a little harder to pin down. It means next, or since, or so. Sometimes people just say "syne" out of the blue, as a sort of, oh well, a sort of sigh. So "Auld Lang Syne" means old long since (or next, or so, or sigh).

The other main event of midwinter in Scotland is the shoot. The shooting season begins in early November and with the approach of Christmas winds up to its grand finale. To our great surprise we were invited to a shoot at Airlie Castle, family seat of the ancient clan of Ogilvy, which David, the romantic dark-haired heir apparent, and his wife, Tarka, an artist, were hosting. John had never expressed any interest in shooting, in fact he is rather disdainful of the sport; the breeding of pheasants for the sole purpose of shooting them disgusts him, and crashing about in the woods seems to him an unnecessary excuse for a convivial male-bonding luncheon afterward. Yet the invitation to Airlie was different, not the least for the unusual aspect of including ourselves, and even Elliot, as they had a boy of their own about the same age.

It turned out that, fond of shooting or not, John had all the requisite gear—tweed shooting jacket with leather elbow patches, baggy moleskin trousers fastened just below the knee ("plus-twos"), heavy socks, cartridge belt, tweed cap, Wellies, and shotgun. Finding the scattered bits and pieces as if he had worn them only yesterday—socks in a drawer here, wool tie in a cupboard there—John dressed with the complete assurance of a man who knew what the occasion called for, for once not seeking a shred of sartorial counsel from me. Indeed I was nearly speechless when he eventually emerged looking like a picture out of a magazine. What I was to wear hardly merited a glance. I was background. John was on parade. We set off on a gray morning, a dusting of snow on the ground, the sun occasionally flickering through a thin cover of cloud.

Airlie Castle is several miles inland from the Guynd, situated in the hilly country of the Angus Glens. One approaches it by way of a curving avenue of beech trees, which dead-ends at the castle wall. Stepping through what was once the portcullis, you find that the castle itself is gone (clan wars) and in its place a graceful Georgian house of pink sandstone rises over a wide lawn and looks out over distant hills. A party of eight was assembled in front of the house, all more or less dressed in the same uniform as John's, and with as many men again in attendance—a keeper and several "beaters" with bright flags to rustle up the game from the underbrush, as well as four or five eager, muddy dogs.

As David divided the party and dispatched the men to various points in the landscape, Tarka and I set off down a steep path into the gorge, our Wellies squelching in the mud, our little boys running ahead toward the riverbank from where we could watch and listen in safety. The keeper was stationed there waiting to ferry members of the party across the river by way of a rowboat rigged up to a pulley (to save the shooters from having to row). There we wives stood shivering and gossiping, wondering where the men were and what was happening, while the boys explored tree roots and dropped stones into the water and we all waited for the sound of a shot.

After about half an hour of this idling we suddenly heard someone shout "Mark!" A clatter of shots resounded through the woods, I couldn't tell from where, then a squawk of a pheasant beating its way furiously across the sky; another shot and down it came in a straight vertical line, landing at our feet. The keeper promptly scooped up the dead bird and stuffed it into his canvas shoulder bag. Then, from behind, a member of the party appeared followed by a beater and a springer spaniel, and with a great flurry of activity all three clambered hastily into the row-boat, the keeper hauled on the pulley, and the boat skimmed over to the other side.

Across the river the dark shapes of hunters emerged against the steep drop of white ground and black trees in flat winter light and I thought of that painting by Brueghel. I am in another land, in another time, I thought briefly. Another shot broke my reverie, then several more, and a pheasant flapping for its life succumbed to its wound and dropped into the river. Immediately a black retriever was dispatched by the keeper, plunging eagerly into the freezing water. The dog quickly made its way to the other side, picked up the bird in his gentle mouth, and swam back. The keeper took the bird still flapping from the retriever, gave it a quick whack on the head with the butt of his gun, and added it to his booty.

Back at the castle a delicious smell of tea and wood smoke greeted us as we sank into friendly old armchairs around the fire. Men in their hunting tweeds bantered jovially about their kill, small hands from below grabbed more than their share of chocolate-covered biscuits off a three-tiered china trolley, the tea slid down and took the chill off our bones, and I was lulled into a kind of stupor of feeling that this scene alone would have been enough of a reason to have made the long flight from New York.

CHRISTMAS EVE DAWNED bright and cold. I pulled aside the heavy curtains and cracked open the wooden shutters in our bedroom. Jack Frost had decorated the insides of our windows in sparkling crystal; I could see my breath in the air. Downstairs Christmas cards littered the mantel piece in the library, a wreath of holly hung on the front door, presents in various states of wrapping were concealed in cupboards, and the turkey was ready to be stuffed. Alison and her youngest, James, were expecting to join us the next day, bringing with them the plum pudding and brandy butter. Yet the house was still bare of tree.

We had discussed and decided where to place the tree. It would occupy a corner of the library, as that would be the warmest place to spend Christmas morning, opening presents by the fire. But the question remained. Where was the tree to come from?

"From the garden, of course," said John.

"Well don't you think we better get started," I asked him early in the day, knowing by now that John could not be rushed. I tried anyway. It was midafternoon and the light was already on the wane when he finally revved up the tractor, hitched up the "bogie" (Scottish for wagon) and we set out down the road between the fields to the garden. The dogs—Foxy and her puppy Sugar—led the way, and Elliot, a little green roly-poly figure encased in goose down, ran along side, kicking at the snow.

In the garden we craned our necks and squinted against the sharp sunlight to appraise the top ten or twelve feet of one tree after another. From forty feet below it wasn't easy. Some seemed lopsided, full on one side and scrawny on another, others bare at the top; still others looked well proportioned but too difficult to get at. At last we settled on what we trusted our eyes to have judged to be both an accessible and well-rounded tree. Elliot and I took our post just inside the garden gate and watched in trepidation. With a methodical swing of the ax, one after another, John cut deeper and deeper into the base of the tree. Finally, with one last push, the trunk cracked and with a stately *whoosh* the tree fell just where he had directed it, toward the side of the garden where it would not be caught by the others. Then he picked up his saw and took off the top twelve feet. On closer inspection it was indeed as full and well balanced and huge a Christmas tree as I could have imagined. We squeezed the branches of our fresh kill through the gate and heaved it onto the bogie, with Elliot chirping and skipping about, overcome with joy and excitement at our triumph over nature.

Back at the house we flung wide the front door and the double doors of the library. Cold air rushed after us as the branches of the tree grazed the stone floor, swept the telephone off the desk, and sent papers flying. Standing straight in its corner the tree tickled the ceiling and reached halfway across the room. The metal tree stand broke under its weight (even John's mother had never dreamed of a tree this size). So after a good deal of muttering and cursing John imported his workbench and an assortment of tools and set to work constructing a stand on the spot while I served as the temporary ballast, swaying between the pine branches and the bookshelves.

By dark we were pulling the boxes of Christmas decorations out of a cupboard in the dining room, gold and silver and red and green shiny balls, garlands of tinsel, and a large box of various pieces made by the Polish refugees during the war: blown eggs brightly painted and tasseled with gold, little birds shaped out of pheasant down strung on silver cords, and weavings of string like spiderwebs with dangling beaded ribbons. Elliot positioned himself high on the ladder, halfway to the ceiling, imagining himself in charge of decorations, ordering up this bauble or that, hardly believing his sudden fortune at having so giant a tree in the house. "Nine Lessons and Carols" came over the BBC, a chorus of boys' voices sang "In the deep midwinter," and two yellow dogs nested together by the fire. The invasion of evergreen spread its branches from the dark corner of the library, twinkling with tiny lights. How fantastic this was! How pagan, this sacrifice of tree! How wonderfully audacious and gorgeously bizarre!

Yet in the midst of our joyous activity a small question continued to haunt me. How many Christmases would we have to spend at the Guynd before we cleared the garden?

SIX

These Woods, These Cultur'd Plains

. . .

MY SENSES HAD A NEW REPERTOIRE. THE BREATH OF honeysuckle at the doorstep, the sweaty-sweet smell of the potato flower wafting across the field, the scent of dry pine needles and sun-baked hay bales. I could smell rain coming. Elliot's ginger hair smelled of fresh air and the bushes he'd been crawling under. I knew when the dogs had been rolling in a dead sheep or in cow dung—I knew the difference. Indoors, I could dissect the inexorable Scottish summer blend of a roasting haunch of venison, ripening peaches, wilting roses, last night's wood smoke, and wet boots on a stone floor.

I knew that it must be about nine in the morning when I heard the sudden swoosh of the postie's van, confirmed by the squeak of his brakes and the babble of his radio jarring the morning quiet as he opened the door of his van, and then the slap of our mail on the doorstep. I listened for the *clickety-click* of the wheat ripening on a dry summer's day. I knew the "kilee kilee" of the oystercatcher circling over the barley, the warble of the dove in the woods, the song of the wagtail, green finch, and coal tit. After dark on a still summer night, if I opened the front door and waited a few moments, there would be the hoot of an owl from across the field.

At a glance I could identify that tree in the distance as a beech or a lime or a chestnut or a Scots pine by its distinctive profile, just as surely as I could tell a Van Gogh from a Matisse, a city bus from a commuter coach, a nickel from a quarter. At the end of a really sunny summer day, the *haar*—a cooling mist—rolls in off the North Sea. If the day was mostly cloudy I would look for the light in the evening when the sun sank low enough to get underneath the clouds and shone with a surreal sideways brilliance, the trees all back-lit as if on a stage. And then maybe a rainbow. On a June night, if the moon was full and the sky clear, around midnight I would look from our bedroom window for the sliver of silver that was the horizon of the North Sea.

As for Elliot, he was growing up country-wise. On his long walks around the circuit with his nanny, Carol, he collected bird feathers and wildflowers—forget-me-not, ragwort, and clover. His fingers knew the velvety coat of a dead mole and the sharp prickles of the gorse bush (that's the stuff Winnie-the-Pooh kept falling into), the shock of stinging nettle on a bare ankle and the balm of dock leaf rubbed against the skin where it burned. He could tell a stalk of wheat from a stalk of barley. He could say "thistle" without lisping.

I continued to be astonished at the variety of valuable natural assets we had at the Guynd. The chanterelles, if you know where to find them in the moss, in the woods, are the rarest of delicacies. Stephen knew where they were hiding. To John's mild irritation Stephen would show up at the front door with his surfeit as an offering—probably about twelve quids' worth if you were to buy them at Harrod's. John never seemed suitably grateful for the gesture, instead fretting that Stephen was stripping the woods of their spores. The elder bush yields a musty, white flower that can be made into a syrup. Throw the heads into a vat of hot water with plenty of sugar and lemons and let it steep for a few days. Strain and top up with soda water. If you could bottle and drink the essence of a summer day, this would be it. Even that loathsome weed the stinging nettle can be made into a delicious soup, if you pick it young enough. And don't forget your gardening gloves.

Commodities that don't appear to be commodities, but are, fall upon the Guynd like gifts from heaven. Like snowdrops. These are the little white bell-shaped flowers that come out in February, no matter what; a floral carpet promising spring, they defied the winter gloom that would actually be with us for many weeks to come. There are masses of them, all along the banks of the Elliot at the bottom of the garden. Like daffodils they seed themselves and spread. One day a man named Lambert came to the door to ask if we would be interested in selling some of our snowdrops. He had traveled all the way up from

Cambridgeshire where he was in the nursery business. John showed him down to the riverbank where he dug up forty or fifty trays of snowdrops, offered us four quid a tray, and paid us on the spot. The following February the snowdrops were in bloom again—you couldn't even tell where Lambert had taken them the spring before—and he came and bought some more. Lambert was followed by another man with a nursery in Fife. This fellow said he'd be sending us a check, that is, unless he'd be passing by this way again soon, in which case he'd bring his check with him. He made off with his snowdrops but we never heard from him again. The mobile phone number he scribbled on the back of a matchbook never picked up. There you have it, a snowdrop thief.

Then there were the ladies from the Edinburgh zoo who turned up looking for bamboo to feed the giant panda bears. This is a rather rare plant to be found in Scotland. From a neighbor of ours the ladies had learned that around the old walled garden we had a lot of bamboo that was lost in the overgrowth, and that we might be agreeable to parting with some of it. They came with their shovels and spades and dug up huge swaths of bamboo by the roots, stuffed them into several large canvas bags, and trucked off to Edinburgh. We didn't even think of asking them for money.

Things grow here, and other people need them. It's just a question of finding the right market. There are the yews, for instance, all needing to be cut back, way back. We learned there was a medical lab in France that was looking for fresh-cut yew to employ in a new cure for cancer. Here's how it goes: If you are pruning your yew hedge, and if you can get your yew clippings into a refrigerated truck within ten hours of cutting them and the truck can reach France in forty-eight hours or less, you'll get thirty-five pence a kilo. Since John doesn't like cutting anything unless he can think of some use for the waste, this one was made for us. Except that after studying the proposition more carefully we realized that they needed the mere shavings off of yews that are clipped annually, while ours are so overgrown we would be cutting off whole branches. It wasn't going to work.

There are the more obvious assets, like the three hundred acres of woodland. The Guynd is the only place in the vicinity of Arbroath with anything like it, which makes it a sanctuary for birds and wildlife. Like Central Park in the midst of New York City, the Guynd is an oasis in a desert of farmland. John's father used to regularly set out with a small shooting party to thin the population of pheasant, woodcock, and hare, and their numbers were dutifully recorded in the house Game Book. But this kind of wild game was becoming quite rare as their habitat was increasingly threatened by modern farming methods.

Instead of an active Game Book we had a shooting tenant, a neighboring farmer named Brunton whose farm is at least five times the size of the Guynd but has no woodland, and therefore little wildlife. Brunton raised his pheasants for shooting at the Guynd. "Industrial pheasants," as John scornfully referred to them. For pheasants, as everyone knows, are not indigenous to Britain. They were introduced from China for the purpose of the shoot. They're coddled with grain and flutter peacefully around in the underbrush until they're old enough to fly into the face of death by gunshot.

Come August, we'd see Brunton almost every day driving through in his Land Rover to check on the wee chicks, enclosed in a pen under cover of a grove of evergreens, feeding on cornmeal. Brunton also employed a gamekeeper, a man named Shaw, to keep the foxes and other predators in check. In the fall Brunton hosted his shooting parties, charging 150 pounds per gun. Around Christmas Eve we could expect to find his offering: a brace of pheasant hooked to the front door.

"Standard," said John, the first time I discovered this sumptuous, nut-brown country still life dangling from the doorknob. "You know how to gut a pheasant?"

"I'll pluck if you gut," I promised.

So after the birds had hung in the root cellar for the requisite couple of days I took them out by the woodpile to pluck. Plucking sounded like fun, but it wasn't. I soon discovered that it was too easy to tear the skin as I tugged the feathers off the bird, and the more I stripped it the less attractive the bird appeared to be, with its wounds exposed and its head dangling pathetically from its broken neck. The dogs sat in rapt attendance as pheasant down blew away in the breeze, and Elliot scooped up the long iridescent tail feathers of the cock. Then I looked up Delia Smith on pot-roasting pheasant in cider, and there was enough dinner for about two of us, so it was just as well that Elliot wanted nothing to do with it. The best part of it was the stock left over from the stewing of the birds, a rich and woodsy nectar that made for the beginnings of a very good soup.

A hundred years ago the woods at the Guynd were entirely hardwood trees—oak and beech—planted for the long term. But the postwar period saw a rising trend in softwoods—larch and spruce—for faster growth and quicker sales. If John's ancestors had known how little profit there was to be made from these trees in the long run, they wouldn't have bothered. Still, occasional timber sales are worth the degrading effects of a logging truck grinding up the roads. One year we sold off a small plantation of conifers up the front drive. But the dead elms, I learned, are far more valuable per tree, especially the burls. This is the gold—the veneer wood—of fine cabinet making.

I first learned about dead elms from Patrick, who showed up at our front door one day, introducing himself as a woodturner. Built like a lumberjack, with sparkling blue eyes and wavy blond hair, he asked in his soft Dundonian accent if there was by any chance some space we could spare in our farm buildings where he might set up a wee workshop. As we stood there on the front doorstep, he noticed a fallen stonework baluster that belonged on the roofline, and a few others missing from above.

"Do you know," he said, picking it up and handling it,

"that if you reproduced this in oak, it would weather just as well as this soft stone?"

I looked interested.

"I know a shipyard in Dundee," Patrick went on, "where they're chucking out old ship masts. Solid oak. I could see if I could get my hands on some, you know?"

Patrick had been supporting himself, he went on, with decorating jobs. And although, he said, he was expecting to move on to woodturning, he could still be persuaded to do a painting job now and then, for a friend. This Celtic god might be a very handy fellow to have around. And pleasant, too, with his innately courteous manner and his cheerful flow of ideas. He had a son the same age as Elliot, I learned, and a daughter. His wife, Nicky, was South African. John would certainly take to a man who thought in terms of recycling materials, like ship masts, I was sure. A man who could improvise, help fix things around the place. Surely we could clear a little space in one of our farm buildings for Patrick and his saw bench, his bandsaw, and his lathe.

Just as I predicted John immediately took to Patrick and to his interest in trees (in fact, John was more comfortable talking to a craftsman like Patrick than he was to most of his fellow gentrymen), and he quickly became a regular for morning coffee. Patrick and John would sit in the kitchen talking about machinery, or about the different qualities of veneer woods—Patrick spoke lovingly with his hands about the creamy browns of walnut or the intricate convolutions of bur elm. A beech tree, he told us, could also be valuable if it was "spolted," that is, when the rot from fungi penetrates into the wood and draws interesting squiggley lines. "Polish that up," Patrick would carry on, rolling a cigarette, "and you're into the dashboard market, custom-built Italian sports cars and the like. Problem is, you can't tell the quality of the spolting from the outside, but only after you've cut a cross section, and believe me, if anyone could figure out how to create this effect, they'd have been doing it long ago. Otherwise beech is as good as firewood."

Then the conversation might drift to the question of where to get the best beer. Or about how to *make* the best beer. Eventually, the morning almost gone, Patrick would be off in his car promising to return in the afternoon to look at that dead tree below the burn, and did we need anything in town. Then we wouldn't see him again for two weeks.

Still, Patrick was so promising. And he had a way of talking confidentially and sympathetically with both John and me, of addressing our differing objectives. He located the urgency of our separate goals and would cannily suggest ways of keeping the one happy while at the same time serving the interests of the other. "Once I get that dead elm out of the den," he'd say to John, "you'll have some beautiful wood for that new kitchen counter," winking at me.

Patrick and I would wander around the house discussing decoration. We talked about color, light, contrast, and the craft of painting. He had practiced all kinds of faux painting techniques. "Do you know how much they would pay me in London to re-create the aged look of this wall color?" he asked, inspecting the sun-stained yellow of an upstairs bedroom. He talked about paint with the same loving intimacy that he talked about wood. "Quality paint," he would say, "is like strong coffee. It takes a lot of cream to diffuse the color."

For me the object of these discussions, as much as they were entertaining, was to coax Patrick into painting the back hall, a job that meant operating from the top of a twenty-foot ladder. He would love to do it, and he promised to get to it between his other obligations, which he was then happy to list along with the various complicated conditions and sets of circumstances that happened to stand in the way just now. Actually pinning Patrick down to any plan of action, I found—and his wife agreed—was like trying to find the end of a tangled string. Patrick, for his part, would argue that talking to John was like searching a library without a catalogue.

In the elaborate plan that would someday lead him to the pastoral life of the woodturner, Patrick would be wielding a chain saw and learning his way through the hazardous byways of the timber business—how to identify good veneer wood on private estates, how to safeguard his arrangement with a private landowner, then how not to be cheated by the middlemen who sell the timber abroad. Veneer wood, I learned, usually ships from the UK to Switzerland to be milled. Between the languishing dens of Scotland and the mighty mills of Switzerland, between a rotten beech tree in the woods and the gleaming dash-board of an expensive sports car, opportunities for deceit and corruption are quite a few.

Before I knew anything about the timber business it seemed amazing that we could be paid something like two thousand pounds to have a dead tree removed from where it was only looking pathetic and in the way. But this was what Patrick promised and, at least once, delivered. The second time he removed an elm he didn't get paid, he said, so neither did we. The dead elm was hauled out and in its wake lay the mangled fence and rutted field that logging vehicles inevitably leave behind. Morag, a tenant who kept her horses in the same field, had to find another place for them until Patrick got around to fixing the fence a few weeks later.

SCOTLAND IS 60 PERCENT the size of England but most of it is rock or moorland. This makes farming in the more fertile areas of the Lowlands intensive and competi-tive, and the farmland of the Guynd—116 acres of arable (about a quarter of the estate as it exists today) its most valuable natural asset by far. This was the real business of the Guynd, its bread and butter.

Until the late eighteenth century being a landowner didn't necessarily mean that you were rich. An estate such as the Guynd was divided into small crofter's partitions, and from the crofters the laird was paid the equivalent of about three shillings an acre, and the pay was usually "in kind," such as in bolls of wheat, trusses of straw, or so many chickens. But after the agricultural improvements in the eighteenth century, the lairds found themselves suddenly rather well off. Under new farming methods such as crop rotation and a greater practical knowledge of the chemistry of crops like the turnip, which replenished the soil with nitrogen, their fields were much more productive. The turnip also made good winter feed for the animals. In the past the Lowland cattle nearly starved over the winter months. In the spring the emaciated herd would stagger back into the fields, and those that could not even stagger were literally carried by men; they called it "lifting day."

A man from Angus and a man from Aberdeenshire combined their breeding stocks to create the Aberdeen-Angus, a fat and fine-boned all-black specimen. These animals fed on summer pastures of nourishing white clover, a crop that, like the turnip, also fed nitrogen back into the land. The arable fields were enlarged and enclosed and demarcated by hedgerows of hawthorn and blackberry. The fields were also drained in a sophisticated plumbing system of underground conduits. Local farmers paid rent to the laird in exchange for their use of the fields, a rent perhaps five times higher than before, and finally now in cash. Meanwhile the laird himself reserved a small piece of his arable land for the "home farm."

With the improvements came an appreciation of natural scenery such as Scotland had never known. It was not until the late eighteenth century that Scotland's misty moors and rocky crags were considered anything but dreadful and threatening. The Scots traditionally built their country houses to turn their backs on nature in every sense, sited primarily for shelter from wind and rain, as near as possible to a thoroughfare or source of water (often the same thing), closely planted with trees and hard by the kitchen garden. The old house by the garden at the Guynd was just such a place. When the first Ouchterlonys built the house, the "low road" passed right below the house along the Elliot Water.

New money and new concepts of beauty in the late eighteenth century exerted a radical influence on the scene. The new mansion house at the Guynd stood proudly and frankly exposed, as far from the public road as possible. At the pivotal center of it all, the house offered a panoramic view of the pastoral scene of peacefully grazing animals in the north, south, east, and west "parks." Now the cattle were kept at a polite distance from the house by a "ha-ha," an invisible trough that enclosed them without the visual interruption of a fence or hedge. The crops were raised in the outer perimeter and comprised a distant view in shades of green to yellow. Beyond the fields the estate was surrounded by a dense plantation of hardwood trees, an asset badly needed in the barren lands of northeast Scotland and which finally the lairds could afford to create.

In the eighteenth century the word *landscape* took on a new meaning. Until then it had meant a painting, but now there was a new breed of professional called the landscape designer, and the material of his art was the land itself. Whereas the painter worked in a studio with brush and canvas, the landscape designer heaved around huge tracts of earth, planted trees in artistic clumps, dug ponds, and redirected rivers—all for the sake of the "landscape," or the living picture. These earthworks were also ingeniously woven into the workings of the farmland or woodland so that they succeeded not only as a thing of beauty but as a source of profit for the landowner.

The landscape that was framed by the windows of the laird's country house was also a gateway to intellectual discussion and philosophic contemplation, an invitation to enter the picture, project himself into its depths, to disappear into the background and melt into the seamless transition between pleasure park, pasture, and woodland. While strolling or riding, this pastoral scene was supposed to free his mind of the petty concerns of the household or farm and allow it to drift creatively and spiritually away with the breezes in a kind of timelessness of pure emotion: gaiety, grandeur, beauty, or melancholy, and, the closer he ventured to the wild, the sublime. Then from a carefully designated spot at some distance from the house, a folly, a temple, or at least a garden seat might be offered so that he could look back at an oblique angle upon the perfect classical proportions of his house, a Greek temple of refinement. There the ladies, dressed in flowing dresses à la Greque reclined on scroll-armed chaise longues, read the poetry of Alexander Pope, and contemplated a landscape painting of the Roman Campagna.

At the time of the improvements these estates were

built by people "who thought they had inherited the world and taken possession of eternity." John Ouchterlony, Esq., had every reason to believe that his newly designed landscape would be nurtured and maintained forever. A tree planted today would shade the next generation of Ouchterlonys, and the next, and the next. Each generation would oversee the planting of more trees, *"with verdure cloth'd,"* each would ensure that the fields were continuously *"stor'd with golden grains."* What could possibly interfere with so perfectly designed and secure a system of agriculture and primogeniture?

Indeed for many years no one could imagine. For most of the nineteenth century there was peace and prosperity in the land. The rents rolled in; the lairds were rich. At the Guynd, in the old days, the gardeners trimmed three acres of lawn by means of a horse-drawn mower and maintained five miles of paths through the woods, around the lake and up to the temple, down to the Elliot Water, on to the garden, across the bridge and back to the road. The improvements to the countryside were complete, and by now the parkland trees mature and stately, the hedgerows thick, and the woodland deep.

TO A GREAT EXTENT the designs and methods of these eighteenth-century improvers are still in place at the Guynd and elsewhere. The fields are cultivated by local farmers, or let by the season for pasture, and the rents still roll in to the laird. But they are no longer enough to sustain a grand house. Furthermore, the designed landscape of the eighteenth century has come under the pressure of the modern British farmer's methods and equipment. On the country roads we regularly slowed to a sedate fifteen miles per hour in the wake of a farmer astride his forklift or towing a sprayer, its extensions folded up like the wings of a giant grasshopper. Miles upon miles of hedgerows throughout Britain have been eradicated for the sake of bigger and faster crop production.

While the hedgerows at the Guynd are still in place, the 400 horsepower tractors the farmers drive make heavy work of the estate roads and, once in the field, their twelve-inch plows dig too deep into the soil and often too close to the roots of ornamental trees. Then the sprayers come over, dousing the field with a lethal dose of chemicals for the sake of a reliable well-rounded potato, and thereby killing off several links in the chain of nature, a host of flora and fauna. And the twenty-foot vans the farmers use to transport their animals in and out of the fields clip the lower branches off the trees along the drives.

John was forever caught between the need to keep the fields worked and the farmers satisfied on the one hand, and the desire to maintain nature's balance and the beauty of the landscape on the other. He would buy all the latest books and devour magazine articles on the subjects of the rape of the land, the corruption of the food business, the debate over organic versus chemical farming. Meanwhile, I would read up on the history of British country life, finding solace in how things used to be, just as the world tends to look tidier from the window of an airplane than from the ground.

All things considered, the Guynd landscape looked good to me. It's basic shape could easily be discerned; it had, as they say, "good bones." But what the Guynd had gained in the maturity of some of its trees it had also lost three-fold in the views that were obviously so much a part of the plan. The view of the North Sea five miles southeast could be had only from upstairs. And the view from the temple of *"yonder mansion"* could only be imagined, as it was now completely obscured by woods. The paths were overgrown, the woods needed thinning, a beloved generation of parkland trees were dying off, and none had been planted to take their place.

As it turned out, I was hardly alone in believing the old days a more perfect time. A number of official agents reinforced the notion that we happened to be sitting on a piece of what is considered to be Britain's most original cultural contribution: the designed landscape, and that we were therefore, like it or not, the stewards of a national treasure.

In the ferment of the preservationist 1970s the Guynd had been included in a study of designed landscapes by an organization called Land Use Consultants, or LUC. Thereafter the Guynd has been listed in an inventory of designed landscapes, a status that made it something akin to a listed building and therefore no longer simply one's own private business. Not long after the LUC people appeared, a professor from the University of Glasgow, one A. A. Tait, included a discussion of the Guynd in his book on Scottish landscapes. Not far behind Tait came Turnbull, a graduate student from Saint Andrews who was writing her thesis on the eighteenth-century landscape designs of Thomas White and Son, of which the Guynd is one example.

Soon the Scottish Garden History Society was in touch, then the Countryside Commission, the Nature Conservancy Council, the Farming and Wildlife Advisory Group, and Historic Scotland. Finally the Royal Commission on Scottish Buildings and Monuments sent two surveyors and a photographer to make detailed architectural drawings and photographs of the Guynd for its files. All of these agencies had a bounty of free advice and expertise to offer, as well as the possibility of partial funding for the restoration of both house and landscape.

My keenest desire was to restore the lake. By far the most ornamental feature of the Guynd landscape the lake, or "loch," as it was called in Victorian times, was first created to drain the fields and later developed into a decorative feature of the park, planted with exotic trees, a virtual arboretum of new world species. The first summer I spent at the Guynd there was still water in the lake, about two inches deep at the near end, and Will Crighton mowed the path around it often enough. The woods around it were alive with the chiffchaff and the magpie; black moorhens squawked and beat a retreat at our approach. A year later I would be carrying Elliot in a backpack around it, brushing past rhododendrons and stinging nettle, harvesting a little wild mint sprouting out of the swamp or wild raspberries on our way. Elliot's little fingers would reach over my shoulder and clip the berries from mine, one by one. We'd cross the arched wooden bridges, three in all, and at the end of the circuit emerge onto an acre of lawn.

I wondered if we could at least clear enough bulrushes out of the lake to win back a little water to row on, or skate on in winter, as John had done as a child. We probably wouldn't be able to return it to the scene where his grandparents held theatricals, when the lawn was clipped right down to the water's edge. But it could still be beautiful, in a wild sort of way.

Christopher, who had been sent over from the Scottish Garden History Society, arrived one fine June day with his Wellies and notebook. I took him around the lake so he could identify the various ornamental plantings and assess its potential for restoration. Like the plant hunters who combed the jungles of the new world a century before him, Christopher now plunged into derelict old world gardens in search of those very same specimens.

"Irish yew here—*Taxus*—you can tell it by its branches that grow upward like this," he said. "But this one is so overgrown it's lost its shape now." Farther down the path he inspected another yew that had become so entangled with a rhododendron nearby that they had finally struck a deal with their branches and become one. "There's a bit of spontaneous grafting!" said Christopher cheerfully. Farther on, "That's a sequoia, or *Sequoiaden-*

dron giganteum. What we call a Wellingtonia here. It's too bad you can hardly see its marvelous shape because of this sycamore in the way," he said, slapping its trunk. *"Aurea marginata* here—that's the holly with the cream edges." He fingered the leaves. "Serbian spruce here. And Chilean pine, otherwise known as a monkey puzzle, of course you know. Very popular with the Victorians."

"Why *do* they call it monkey puzzle?" I asked, once and for all.

"There are a variety of answers to that question," answered Christopher. "One is that the branches kind of swoop down like monkey tails, slightly curled at the end."

"That explains the monkey part, but not the puzzle."

"The puzzle is well . . . a puzzle," said Christopher, marching on. "These along the edge are alders. They might have been planted to keep the banks from eroding. But they also tend to voluntarily populate distressed areas and in this case they've obviously proliferated out of control."

Something in the middle of the lake caught Christopher's eye and he suddenly plunged into the thicket of bulrushes and wild yellow iris, fighting his way to a clump of growth. I had no choice but to follow him. "Ah, I thought so," he said with a sigh of satisfaction, as we struggled onto higher ground. "This was once an island." A large stone urn lay on its side in the grasses, and a pair of yews grew haywire. "In the old days this would have been a point of interest, or perhaps the romantic destination of a little rowboat ride. Look, there's your boathouse right over there," he said optimistically, ignoring the jungle of stinging nettle around it. "Shall we have a peek inside?"

A few weeks after Christopher's visit we received a wonderful four-page letter from him describing every aspect and component of the Guynd landscape—its historical context, its character and value, its highlights, the main objectives in restoring it stage by stage, prescriptions for its maintenance in the future. He characterized these prescriptions as either 1) urgent, 2) necessary, or 3) desirable. (If only, I thought, somebody could map out my own life with such confidence and clarity.) Christopher also suggested that we might apply for a grant through the Farming and Wildlife Advisory Group, or FWAG.

It wasn't difficult to get a grant for FWAG's advice, which consisted of an all-day meeting at the house with two outdoorsy bureaucrats. They came with booklets and brochures and reports on other estates with successful restoration schemes. As John and I led them on a thorough tour of the farm and woodland, they took copious notes. A few weeks later came the report and the proposal of a plan. They suggested that we create "grass margins" around our cereal fields to accommodate a greater variety of wildlife. We should create a "species-rich" grassland for the animals pastures—that is, mixed, organic—though this, they admitted, might put off the commercial farmers. They were also very keen to see the lake restored as a wildlife habitat.

While we were really only interested in dredging the

lake and cutting back the growth, the people of FWAG had more ambitious plans. In order to justify their employment and make use of their extensive training, they stood by a strict mandate of historical correctness. In the case of the lake this would mean eradicating the rhododendrons—at least the purple ones—known here derisively as *ponticum*, "an invasive species," and furthermore not a native of Scotland—that should be done away with. For that matter, most of the plantings around the lake, if not invasive, were not native either. How, anyway, was one supposed to identify the correct historic moment? Why couldn't it be 1936? Or 1955?

On top of these imponderables we had to consider the side effects of being funded, such as the bureaucrats showing up on the doorstep every so often to make sure that we were following the prescribed plan, and then presenting us with another load of paperwork. While they appeared to be supporting the landowner, I couldn't help but wonder if they were even more concerned about supporting the system that appeared to be supporting the landowner. Furthermore, their plan might be at odds with the landowner's personal interests and priorities. It also might be at odds with the objectives of another agency or interest group offering their free advice. Pretty soon John and I were weighing the urgency of dredging the lake against the twenty-five other problems we had to solve, and the subject was tabled for the time being.

How I longed for the simplicity of rural America, where a farm is simply a farm, and where woods are just plain woods. I recalled the wisdom of an American land-scape designer. "You know," he said to me, "sometimes all you really have to do is define a path, and the wildness just falls into place around it."

IT WAS AN AMERICAN COUPLE, houseguests and old friends of mine from San Francisco, who finally got us going on the biggest landscape project we had ever tack-led.

Over the years, houseguests had come in all varieties, but I could divide them roughly into two basic types. The first type wanted to come and inspect the Guynd, go sight-seeing by day, come back for tea, perhaps a game of cro-quet on the lawn before dressing for dinner at eight. They basked in a real-life fantasy that they were staying in a grand old country house, if a bit dilapidated, and they were lucky enough to be friends of the people who owned it. Meanwhile I enjoyed playing the host to this fantasy, because it was my fantasy too. These visits were preceded by a flurry of polishing and dusting around the main rooms, and frantically reducing the buildup of tools, elec-trical parts, and unopened mail that had taken up residence on the hall table. I hung the fresh towels in their room, satin-cushioned hangers in the cupboard, and selected the latest issue of *Heritage Scotland* for the bedside table. Downstairs I laid the table with silver and glass, filled the ice bucket, switched on the picture lights, and pretended for a moment that someone else was minding the roast in the kitchen. On departing, our guests would sign the book, glowing with compliments, and as they drove away I felt the distinct satisfaction that we had added a page to their store of memorable travel experiences, of amusing tales of their privileged insight into country life in Scotland.

The second type of houseguests came to get their feet wet and their hands dirty. They ignored John's protests and beat us to the washing up in the morning, they explored the basement with as much interest as any other part of the house, they prowled John's workshop in search of gardening tools and plunged headlong into the underbrush. They didn't just bring their ideas—*everybody* had ideas, and they were all sure they were the first people to think of them—these were the houseguests who brought their bodies to the job and got it done. Peter and Cenita were of this second variety.

"If only you could see the fields from the front doorstep," lamented Cenita, who was a practicing landscape designer. "That laurel hedge should never have been allowed to grow so high."

I fully agreed with her. Furthermore, it was one of the items on the Scottish Garden History Society's to-do list. But I had to offer that John had justified the hedge's overbearing height by arguing that it served as a wind barrier.

"Nonsense! Not at that distance. It's at least forty feet from the house!" The longer she looked at it, the more impassioned Cenita became about eliminating the hedge from her view.

With perfect timing, John's nephew Pete arrived for a

visit from Canada, looking for some hard physical labor to keep himself fit. Cenita's husband Peter was also itching for the chance to pitch in to a meaningful project, and with a lot of good-natured banter, and Cenita and I chiming in with encouragement, Peter and Pete managed to persuade John to lend them a couple of chain saws and they set to work. When the first window on the grazing animals and the sweep of green pasture opened up in the hedge, we all knew there was no turning back. Down they came, one twenty-foot laurel after another; the dramatic progress created a momentum that was irresistible. Peter and Pete worked long hours.

"This is really hard on the chain saws," said John.

By the end of four long days the view opened up like something out of the sketchbook of Capability Brown. Light glowed through the front windows of the house with greater brilliance than ever, while heaps of felled laurels over the drive left just enough room for a single vehicle to turn around. Elliot and Stephen's daughter Gwen threw themselves into the deep piles of brush and dug tunnels underneath them, leading to secret hideouts.

"It's going to be a job cleaning this lot up," said John.

Now Cenita was looking critically at the four lopsided yews that stood alone in front of the row of laurel stumps. She tried to be kind, to think of some decorative role they might play; she wondered if they could be effectively cut and shaped but then promptly gave up. "It's no use, they're too far gone, you've got to get rid of them too."

This only helped to confirm John's Sisyphean theory

about landscape work—that one job only shows up the glaring need for another. Sometimes it's better to leave well enough alone.

"That's a winter job," said John, desperately looking for a way to halt the project.

Over the next few months, Peter and Cenita having long since returned to California, John lifted one bogey load of felled laurel after another and dumped the brush at the edge of the woods half a mile from the house. Later still, when it was dry enough, Stephen burned the rest. The following summer a neighboring farmer who owned an excavator dug out the laurel stumps. He also uprooted the yews, which, having stared at them for a few months, John was finally ready to sacrifice. Then he bought a twenty-pound bag of grass seed. We spread it around the newly liberated strip of lawn in front of the house and watered it every day that it didn't rain.

"Aren't you pleased?" I asked John when the new grass began to sprout, and not a trace of a stump could be detected.

People came over and noticed that something was different, very different, but they couldn't exactly tell what it was, just that it was better. I had a new feeling for Capability Brown's seamlessly deceptive landscape makeovers, much as an oil painter might block out an area of his composition and fill it in somewhere else. So you think you recall seeing some trees there? You must have been dreaming.

How could John deny the extraordinary change we

had made? Now his ancestors' house stood in perfect harmony and communion with nature, just as it was designed to be. The view from the Guynd was a glorious panorama of pasture and farmland, and from far across the fields you could see the house rising "in simple taste," prevailing over its landscape.

"It was a hell of a diversion," answered John, sighing. "Isn't there anything we can do with those laurel poles? It seems such a waste."

SEVEN

Home Economics

...

THE SCOTS ARE FAMOUS FOR THEIR FRUGALITY. The reason for this is simple. Even a rich Scot feels poor compared with his neighbors to the south. And it has always been so. When Boswell took Johnson on a tour of the Highlands and the Hebrides, he was at pains to make his English friend comfortable amid conditions so primitive the latter had not believed them possible in the civilized eighteenth-century world. They traveled roads that were no more than dirt tracks across marsh and moor, they stayed in thatched hovels with nothing but a hole in the roof for a chimney, and downed quantities of whisky in order to stomach their meals of gruel and sleep on beds of straw. Hardly a tree was to be seen on this barren landscape. Miserable grain crops competed with hardier weeds in the crofter's little slice of land. So one learns to appreciate the native frugality within the context of generations upon generations of people born to poverty, and understand why the Scots might be inordinately grateful for small things and careful with what they have. When times are hard the Scots are better prepared for them than most of us, for a life of hardship is never buried too deep in the Scottish memory.

This is hardly the land of temptation. I have saved many a quid and many an hour as a result of the utter lack of shopping excitement to be found in the streets of Arbroath. Approaching the town from the west, the clay-red carcass of the Arbroath Abbey looms over the town from its highest point. This medieval relic fell violently to ruins during the Reformation, and still stands gaunt and determined lest we forget Scotland's many battles and disappointments. Just down from the abbey at the top of the High street, a quiet souvenir shop peddles the usual tartan baubles. Farther down lie a Save the Children charity shop, a U Pay Less clothing store, Boots the chemist, KwikPrint, Woolworth's, Victoria Wine, a pet shop, a fishmonger, a woolen shop filled with acrylics in pastel colors, and something called Carpet Disco. I kept meaning to find out what a carpet disco was, exactly.

Everybody on the street looks about sixty, slightly stooped and gray-haired, and they all wear the same sorts of clothes—skirts cut just below the knee, tidy rain jackets—in shades of beige. The clock stopped about 1950. If they aren't sixty they're sixteen—strolling girls in leatherette jackets and loud makeup, frowning girls in T-shirts pushing babies in strollers against the wind, callow youths with round shoulders and spiky hair and pierced eyebrows, hanging around the pay phone, smoking. They looked at me strangely, dressed as I was for the country in my jeans, mud-splattered mac, and Wellies. This, I kept forgetting, was the town.

No pub beckons you inside with a brightly painted sign announcing "The Red Lion," or "The Ram's Head," or "The Pig and Whistle," as they do in England. No window-box a riot of gay-colored petunias and tresses of ivy. There are thirty-two pubs in Arbroath, but their street profile is more like that of a speakeasy. The doors remain shut, even when the pub is open, and it will stay open until the last man leaves. Drinking is a serious occupation in Scotland and there's no need to waste money on a sign.

If the Scots are frugal there is none more frugal than John. It's not so much that he is averse to buying things, but that he will never throw anything away. "Trash," "rubbish," and "garbage" are simply not words in his vocabulary, except when he accused me of "creating trash," which would not exist, you see, if I wasn't creating it. There is compost. There are combustibles. There are recyclables. And there are little plastic yogurt pots that are none of the above but which are very good for mixing up glue. And there are edible substances that cling stubbornly to their jars. "There's loads of stuff left here," he'd say, handing back what seemed to me a very empty jar of Marmite. "Rinse it out in boiling water and you'll have a fine soup stock." One day, he presented me with a pair of my old tights that I had thrown out because they had ladders up and down and holes in the heels. "Did you know that we use these to filter paint?" he asked me, pointing out once again my pathetic wastefulness.

Trash was a more complicated subject than I had ever imagined. How was I to know that a shard of gilded wood was deliberately resting nearby the picture frame it had broken off of, waiting to be glued; that a yellowing newspaper clipping lying about was intended for somebody in particular, once their address was found?

Throwaways that come free and frequently, like wine corks, or computer discs inviting you to twenty free hours of e-mail, John collected in piles somewhere while he considered the possibilities of their transformation—a cork-lined tray, perhaps, or a string of glittering discs to hang in the garden to scare away the crows. You never know.

Elliot rapidly developed the mind and eye of the scavenger. On the city street he would stop short in his tracks, arrested by the sight of some shining little thing on the sidewalk that I, in my insensitive way, had just walked over. Without a word he would pluck it off the ground and stuff it in his pocket—a roll of foam rubber, the wire spring of a ballpoint pen, a broken key ring, the inside guts of a golf ball—already conjuring with its possible function among his toys, or simply because it was a curious thing that might bear closer inspection.

The disposal of trash is as abhorrent a concept to John as the keeping of trash is to some of us. This is a man who will put aside a shattered wineglass with all its pieces, expecting to mend it someday, a man who will dissect a butter wrapper, lifting the foil from the greaseproof paper in order to dispose of its two parts separately, responsibly. This is a man who can admire the molded plastic packaging of a toy tractor for as long as his son admires the toy. He takes pity on everything. For John is interested in how *everything* is made and, once it is made, it seems criminal to dispose of it in so callous a way as so many of us do. Most of all, he believes that for everything he gives up he should get something in return. Was this Scottish, I wondered, or was it just John?

Out in what used to be the stable behind the house was a collection of waste paper, which John had been contributing to for some time. Unaware of this collection, when I first started gathering up the old copies of *National Geographic* and *House and Garden* that were piled high in various corners of the house and stacked them into several knee-high towers on the front steps, it was my understanding that we would be taking them to the dump in Arbroath. Oh no, said John. We're storing it, until the price of paper goes up again. Then we'll sell it. But of course.

I let this one go for a while, but curiosity got the better of me and I eventually decided to call up the Environmental Health Department to ask if there was any interest in our hoard.

"Sure, that's no problem, whereabouts are you staying?"

"We're just five miles west of Arbroath," I answered, and then geared up my courage to ask this reasonable-sounding person how much he would pay us for our trash.

There was a pause while the environmental health

officer revised his mental image. "Exactly how much waste paper have you got there?"

"I'd say a good truck load," I told him.

"Would you say—a ton?"

I wasn't absolutely sure. Could be more. If we could get the paper to the recycling plant in Aberdeen, the officer explained, they'd pay us twelve quid a ton. But if we just wanted it collected, the council would take care of it for us, free of charge.

This seemed a reasonable enough deal to me, if waste paper was worth only twelve quid a ton.

"That's not much," said John when I broke the news. "The price is sure to go up again. Recycling is the wave of the future, what else?"

As I perceived it, *stuff*—of every description—was the most prickly and intransigent obstacle in the way of progress at the Guynd. Long-ago household things were labeled and put away in trunks in the basement, careful inventories were kept of what was what and where. By the time I arrived at the Guynd the basement storage was nearly impenetrable, a towering mess of old mattresses and kitchenware, slipcovers, moldy magazines, stuffed animals missing limbs and busted at the seams, spilling their guts. To my mind, the space itself was more valuable than the stuff that was keeping it from being used, while to John's mind saving for a rainy day (and there are a lot of those in Scotland) was the essence of progress. To have things "in hand" was the idea; whether it was an extra can of plum tomatoes in the kitchen cupboard or the odd nut or screw he'd lifted off the road or saved from something he'd taken apart, he adhered to the philosophy that you never knew when and what you were going to need out here in the country. You had to know how to improvise. To make do with what's available.

The trouble was that there was virtually no available storage space left in the house. The basement rooms had been largely given over to the East and West flats, leaving the wine cellar, game cellar, and housekeeper's room, but they were full of lamps and pictures and furniture. The cook's room, tucked away up its own stone stairway between the first and second floors, had also been taken over with an indecipherable overflow, including a crusty inflatable life raft. There wasn't even enough space for me to store my own clothing. In our bedroom, instead of a built-in closet there was a large piece of furniture known as a "press," and now I knew why—the doors would not shut unless you *pressed* the hangers in sort of sideways. Did people have narrower shoulders when these cup-boards were designed in the 1860s? Smaller hangers? Anyway, all of them were chock-full. Which perhaps explained why John had developed the habit of simply dropping his clothes on the floor.

Vintage clothing occupied most of the other presses in the house: John's flared trousers from the early seventies, jackets with Nehru collars, a stash of moth-eaten weavings from his travels through South America. There were John's and Angus's striped flannel prep school pajamas with name tags sewn into the collars, white woolen undershirts, and a multitude of worn canvas tennis shoes; his father's woolly undershirts and his custom-knit knee socks with the big toe separated from the rest, as a thumb is in a mitten, darned and darned again; Doreen's hats, her little velvet chemises for evening, and her sturdy tartan skirts. And in spite of my mother's efforts earlier on to purge the downstairs cloakroom, we retained a drab assortment of rain gear nobody ever touched—I think they were arthritically frozen onto their hooks—and a small army of Wellington boots in various sizes, which might be useful, that is, if you could match them up.

I did mention to John my first summer at the Guynd that I would be needing a little space for my clothes. But my suggestion that this old coat or that old shirt might be passed along to the needy was inevitably met with protest. After that, I occasionally attacked the overflow in a fit of rebellion and assembled a bagful for the charity shop or, in worse condition, the recycling center. Often as not, before I got the bag safely out the door and into the trunk of the car, John arrested me mid-flight and demanded a review of its contents. Just to make his point, he would extract from the pile this or that item and extol its virtues as a drop cloth or dog blanket, before leaving me in utter disgust to pick up the scattered remains.

No wonder there is a tradition of women in big houses like the Guynd to reserve a room of their own for sulking in. The "sulking room." (*Boudoir*, a lady's chamber, derives from the French *bouder*, to pout, to sulk.)

My problem was confined not to the things that were

enclosed in pieces of furniture but to the furniture itself, which there was too much of. For not only did the house come with a quantity of inherited furniture, John's mother used to pass the dark winter days by frequenting the local auction rooms and was unable to resist a bargain. Sometimes she acquired a piece without in fact meaning to. While waving her paddle to a friend across Taylor's auction room in Montrose one day, she inadvertently placed the winning bid on an enormous "Scotch chest." To justify the acquisitive urge and the occasional accident, Doreen figured that the East and West flats needed furnishing. In fact they were more than amply furnished, and the overflow had migrated upstairs.

One day, freshly inspired to make my point, I counted up all the side chairs in the house and found that they numbered seventy-two. Then, having made the inventory, I started editing, stashing various bits of furniture that seemed to me odd or among the excess into a little-used bedroom and closed the door. But this only solved one problem by creating another.

The laundry presented another challenge. There was the twin-tub "portable" washing machine on wheels, parked in the passage, which rolls into the kitchen to be hooked up to the plumbing in the sink. Mostly we used the other washing machine, out in the garage next to the tractor mower; salvaged from a bygone tenant, it wheezed and grunted and often stalled mid-cycle for no discernible reason. At the end of this grueling performance, it was a short walk around the back to the "drying green," a bit of lawn sheltered by a beech hedge with some washing lines strung between various wooden posts. It followed that the washing must wait for fine weather because a tumble dryer was of course out of the question. If wet weather persisted the laundry could be slung over the line in the linen cupboard, which also housed the electric water heater and was therefore relatively warm and dry. I eventually ceased to dispute these methods and simply left the laundry to John.

There was a collection of housecleaning equipment worthy of a museum. At the top of the back stairs a little army of brooms and other long-handled instruments were lined up on hooks against the wall. I especially liked the telescopic handled brush for reaching the cobwebs at the high corners of rooms. We had a variety of vacuum cleaners parked in unexpected places. One, a cylinder type, was balanced on top of a cupboard in the passage, an upright model stood around the corner, another especially ancient one was carefully stored in its original navy blue box in the cloak room. And there was a small gadget that appeared to be an ancestor of the Dustbuster, which John's mother liked to use on the staircase. The trouble was that none of this equipment really worked. When Kathy first came out from the village to clean she packed her own Electrolux. When she found herself overscheduled two years later, our slot was the first to be dropped. Kathy kindly found us a substitute, but the young woman lasted only one session, phoning up just minutes before she was due the next week to tell me in a terrified voice that she just wasn't up to the job. I suspect that, among other things, she didn't like cleaning the bathtub, as John had firmly instructed her to do, with kerosene (detergent ruins the enamel). The next recruit took one look at the house and on the spot developed a prohibitive case of high blood pressure.

Left to my own devices, and having pleaded long enough with John about the state of our cleaning equipment to no avail, I slipped out to Arbroath one day, ostensibly just to do the usual grocery shopping, and came home with a brand-new Electrolux. John was not impressed with my purchase, even though it was on special, mainly because my brand-new Electrolux required the use of a throwaway bag. All that mattered to me was that its performance, while not brilliant, was noticeably better than anything in the vintage collection. I used it furtively, when John was out of the house, or at least on another floor.

Our housecleaning differences were finally reconciled with the help of a third party by the name of Dyson. I discovered this tall, handsome blond maverick on a train ride to Edinburgh, smiling at me from the pages of my free copy of *Live Wire*. This rather smug-looking fellow had apparently invented a bagless vacuum cleaner, which not only eliminated the waste of paper bags but did a much more effective job of cleaning than any other machine on the market. As the article stated in no uncertain terms, the Dyson was "the only vacuum cleaner in the world to maintain 100% suction, 100% of the time." John had heard of Dyson and actually approved of his invention and, to cut a long story short, a few months later, he bought one, new (secondhand Dysons were extremely hard to come by). The really seductive thing about these machines, I soon discovered, was that the cylinders are transparent, so that as you make your rounds through the house you actually witness the dust being inhaled by its voracious nozzle and spun at top speed into a soft gray pile within. So there's sort of a dialogue with the machine that spurs you on and makes you want to feed it. Those happy Brits who have converted are so smitten that I have even heard them talk about their Dysons at dinner parties.

Perhaps not since the advent of the Aga stove has a piece of household equipment inspired such devotion in Britain. The Aga—it's very name is like a country wife's mantra—is that ubiquitous piece of kitchen equipment perfectly suited to the climate and culture of rural life in Great Britain and apparently of little use anywhere else.

The tradition of large, chilly houses that the natives pretend to enjoy is in fact relatively new. A hundred years ago a large house like the Guynd would have been kept at a comfortable temperature throughout the year. Every room, including the servants' quarters, had a fireplace, and every hearth was regularly stocked with coal. Approaching the house one would have seen smoke billowing forth from several of the twenty-six chimneys at once, and a well-stoked coal stove in the front hallway welcomed the wet and weary at any hour of the day. Every morning the housemaids swept the hearth and stoked it up clean, beat the cushions and wiped the tabletops of yesterday's coal dust.

Eventually the cost of servants made coal heating unaffordable in a large house, for the job was too great without them, but the cost of oil or gas made central heating correspondingly extravagant, not to mention the daunting cost of installing the system. What was the native to do but head for the kitchen? What, indeed, when the postwar British housewife was spending most her day there anyway?

Briefly, the Aga is a cast-iron range that runs perpetually and very economically, whether its fuel is oil, gas, or solid (wood or coal). It not only radiates heat in the kitchen itself, it is also designed to be hooked up to the water-heating system. So that in the Aga-equipped country kitchen, while you're baking the scones for tea in one oven, warming the plates in another, simmering your Aberdeen-Angus beef stew on the range, and drying the laundry you've just brought in from the rain on a pulley line high above your head, while the dogs hog the warmest spot next to the stove and upstairs your houseguest is enjoying a hot bath, this entire carousel of luxury is executed for a few pence worth of energy per day. While all other aspects of mechanical energy in the Scottish household are flicked on and off with regimental frugality (lights never burn in an empty room, and even the electric outlets themselves are switched off when the current isn't needed) the wonderful Aga is always pumping away, reliable as a heartbeat.

Yet defying all tradition, household logic, and rural economy, there was no Aga at the Guynd. In the 1960s when John's father moved the kitchen from the basement upstairs to the main floor and took over a row of pantries, he masterminded its renovation with his usual frugality. Though in the long run the Aga would have saved him money in fuel, in the short run the outlay of serious cash for the equipment no doubt put him off. So the kitchen, which is on the north side of the house, cool even on a warm day in July, was virtually unheated. The stove was electric, and the fridge, a little pantry-sized outfit, was almost unnecessary given the temperature of the room itself. There was no table and no chairs, just a couple of stools on which to perch at a narrow blue Formica counter where, with my back to the window and face to the wall, I could bang my head against the pots and pans hanging on hooks from the shelf above as I tucked into my cock-a-leekie soup.

A glance at the collection of cookbooks suggested that, under the circumstances, John's mother was unenthusiastic about working in the kitchen—*The I Hate to Cook Book* and *How to Cheat at Cooking* are two such titles. Furthermore, it was clear that she labored under a strict postwar regimen of thrift and the salutary advice of *Frugal Food* and *The Pauper's Cookbook*. John continued to spout wisdom from these volumes, such as how to clean the silver in a bath of aluminium and soda, or suggesting that I fry the French toast in lard rather than in butter. "I like the taste of butter," I would venture to remind him, without adding that I detest the taste of lard. He'd give up with a sigh on that morning, try again the next.

The subject of kitchen improvements had caused enough conflict between us. We had already spent more than enough time on the subject of dish traffic flow (whether they should pile up to the left of the sink and move right, or to the right of the sink and move left; I advocated left to right, John right to left) without adding to these debates our even more impassioned feelings about the Aga. But as I faced the prospect of spending one more winter at the Guynd, I knew that we couldn't survive without one. Everyone I knew with a large house had an Aga, and they all swore by them.

John admitted that we needed a warmer kitchen but insisted, like his father, that an Aga was too expensive. Instead he was threatening to outwit us all by installing something called a Bosky, which he had found advertised secondhand in *The Courier*. A distant cousin of the Aga, the Bosky performed the same functions; the difference was it did so by burning wood. "We have three hundred acres of woodland out there," John sternly reminded me. "A fallen tree or two will provide enough fuel for the entire winter." I just didn't understand the economy of the countryside.

That old American adage "Time is money" didn't seem to fly here. The firewood may have been free but it was hardly free of labor. My mind drifted to the cave of logs in a windowless section of the back buildings from whence every evening came the thunk of John's ax splitting wood. The fruits of that effort would be nearly gone by the time we retired from fireside to bed. The Bosky would need refueling throughout the day. Then there was the mess to think about, the variable temperature, the safety. I couldn't imagine why we would put ourselves through this unnecessary hardship.

"What about moving the logs into the kitchen?" I asked John, tracing in my mind the long, circuitous route from the woodshed. "Out of the shed, into the basement door, through the basement, up the stairs. That's a lot of work every day."

John had already figured it out. "I'm designing a pulley system that goes straight from outside the shed, across the yard, and through the window on the back stairs." Very pleased with this scheme, he was at work on detailed drawings, measurements, and calculations on the backsides of business letters and used envelopes, diagrams with numbers and arrows, rubbed out and rewritten here and there, and drawings of pulleys and wheels, all indecipherable to me. "This is something I've been meaning to do for ages."

Even when my mother offered to pay for a brand-new Aga, its hefty price including its elaborate installation, even after the Aga engineer had visited to make sure it could be installed, that it could fit with the existing plumbing and chimney, and had explained all its virtues, which I'd already memorized, even after countless discussions with sensible Scottish friends on the topic (It's essential, especially with a child in the house, said Keith and Elizabeth. If I were you I'd move the whole kitchen into the dining room and start over, said Rita), John was immovable. By the end of the summer the subject of the Aga had become a point of honor that I had lost all hope of shaking. The problem, I decided, was clearly not with Scotland but with John.

With Elliot I left for a three-week stay in New York in October, dreading our return. In the comfort of our little apartment I reveled in the hiss and clang of our over-worked radiators, made a fire purely for the aesthetic pleasure of it, and lolled about in a cotton jersey, my utter peace disturbed only by the occasional rumble of the auto-matic ice-making machine, as I contemplated our marital predicament. If being married to John had not necessarily made me more thrifty, it had perhaps made me slightly more mechanical. I was now more likely to read the instruction pamphlet (or some of it) when something was new, for instance. I might even consider how to fix it if it was broken. I was beginning to appreciate how a thing was made, and how it worked, not just how it looked, or if it was clean. I believed I had earned my Aga.

Meanwhile back at the Guynd John hinted that some-thing was happening that would please me. Anyway it cer-tainly seemed to be pleasing him.

"What would that be?" I asked skeptically, over the transatlantic phone line.

"A Rayburn," he answered, meaningfully.

"What's a Rayburn?"

"It's an Aga, really, only it's better, actually. You can control the temperature. It has a gauge."

"Where did you get it?"

"It was out in the back. Angus bought it off somebody years ago."

"Does it *work?*" was all I wanted to know.

"With any luck, I can get it to work."

John really thrives on suspense of this kind.

When Elliot and I returned in late October, sure

enough, there was the Rayburn. With the help of a neighbor John had maneuvered it into the kitchen, where he was intending to restore it and hook it up to the chimney, the oil supply, and the water tank. The fact that it wasn't yet functioning didn't seem to worry him, as he was now in the midst of other, more urgent projects. The fact that the Bosky had also come to stay, occupying the last corner of unused space in the passage between the dining room and the kitchen, didn't worry him either. Might be a good backup. Until then the oven would make a good place to store broken china.

We were expecting American guests for the Thanksgiving holiday, Katya and Joe from Los Angeles. I had warned them that late November was about the worst time of year to come, but they were not deterred. The heat was of course not turned on (never before December first, as you will recall) and, even though that was only three days away, at the Guynd, as I tried to explain to Katya and Joe, it was not just a matter of flicking the switch. The boiler had to be cleaned, various parts replaced. John would get to it once he'd finished with the Rayburn. "Can I help?" Joe almost pleaded. Unfortunately, he couldn't. Katya came to the dinner table in a hat, and I lent her my old L.L. Bean down-filled vest, which I think she might have also worn to bed.

With miraculous timing, John got the Rayburn humming Thanksgiving morning. He was fairly giddy with delight at his accomplishment, beaming goodwill upon family and friends just in time for the feast, much of which we cooked on the Rayburn, and we all put up a brave show of eating in the dining room, scantily warmed by a small electric heater. From then on, everyone hung out in the kitchen. All day. Unless they were trying to read in bed under an eiderdown.

It finally dawned on me why John had resisted the Aga so adamantly. It was simply unthinkable for him to allow another engineer into our house. It was as unthinkable as allowing another man into our bed. The house was his mistress, and no other man was invited to tinker with it, especially if it had anything to do with the plumbing.

Now I had to adapt to another way of cooking. To slow way down, to plan way ahead. The Aga (or Rayburn) is the opposite of the microwave. You can put a potato in the oven at tea time and have it for supper four hours later. Keep a stew simmering on the top range and leave the house for a two-hour walk. Keep the kettle full of water on the range all night long and in the morning it will be just on the brink of boiling for that first pot of tea. The lower oven, which hums along at about 200 degrees, is just right for warming the plates, also for meringues, I am told, though I've yet to get the hang of meringues in any oven. Most reassuringly, it is nearly impossible to ruin anything with this kind of appliance, unless you forget about it for a day or two, which *is* possible, with often fascinating results. I discovered, for instance, that a potato baked for three or four days will come out hard as a rock on the outside and hollow as a balloon within.

The Scottish diet is historically sticky. Devised from a narrow range of crops to fill the stomachs of hard laborers, bulk traditionally took precedence over taste. Oats were the staple ingredient and oatmeal was the staff of life. As Samuel Johnson put it, "A grain, which in England is generally given to horses, but in Scotland supports the people." The Scots are credited with inventing porridge oats, as well as the more obscure oatcake, which is not a cake at all but a hard, dense, oaty biscuit, which tastes nice in Scotland but personally does not tempt me anywhere else. For luxury, the Scots invented shortbread, which is not a bread at all but again a hard, dense biscuit, this time packed with butter and sugar, quite delicious when the mood strikes. But the greatest gift of Scottish food to my mind is the smoked fish. Being a seaside town, Arbroath had its own local specialty, the Arbroath smokie. This is a pair of haddock, their tails tied together with string so that they can hang on a stick over a barrel of smoking wood chips and sawdust. Many hours later the skin of the Arbroath smokie will be leathery and its insides tender, white, and delicious. Some people buy a pair from the fishmonger, sit on a bench at the dock, and eat smokies right out of their skins with their fingers. Others take them home and make them into "pies" topped with mashed potato, or pâtés mixed with generous amounts of butter. Varieties of smoked haddock and other fish go into the famous "cullen skink," a hearty soup of fish, onions, potatoes, and milk not unlike a New England clam chowder. I devised my own cullen skink with smoked mackerel, and a pâté of Arbroath smokie—American-style, mixed up with a squeeze of lemon juice, a couple of cloves of garlic, and a generous dollop of Hellmann's mayonnaise.

I tried haggis once, I had to. John deplored the dish and insisted that if I must try it, "get it from Fleming's," the reputable butcher in Arbroath. This famous Scottish dish consists of various animal innards ground up with a quantity of oatmeal, stuffed into the lining of a sheep's stomach and tied with butcher's string. Being one of those people who is unafraid of offal, I was not deterred by the haggis description. Yet even having obtained it from Fleming's, and having steamed it for the recommended half hour, when we sat down to eat I had to confess that it tasted like dog food. "I told you," said John.

It is well known that the only way to properly appreciate a haggis is at a Burns night supper. In the dank and dark of a Scottish late January, when the weather is at its most *dreich* (wet, foggy, dark, depressing; there's no exact translation for this word in any other language as there are few places that produce its particular effect), the faithful gather to read aloud from the poetry of the man who wrote "Auld Lang Syne." Around the table they await the great event of the haggis, which, to accentuate the drama, is traditionally "piped in," that is, serenaded by a bagpiper, and addressed with the words of "Bobbie" Burns. Plenty of "champit neeps and tatties" (mashed turnips and potatoes) accompany the bag of boiled guts, and a tumbler of neat single-malt washes the whole mess down; then you get to look forward to another whole year without it.

WE MUST NOW LEAVE the subject of food and return unhappily to the irksome question of how to deal with the accumulation of stuff at the Guynd. As the tension of John's and my own opposing views wore deep grooves in the road of our marriage, as we came to accept these differences as fact, we were nonetheless vigilant in fighting for our sides. Indeed with every inch of space won, I looked ambitiously toward the next mile.

Some five years into our marriage an opportunity arose to rid the house and farm buildings of some excess furniture. Bonham's, the London-based auction house, was organizing something called a "stately attic sale" to be held not far from the Guynd at a huge country house by the name of Fasque, home of the Gladstones of prime ministerial fame. The Gladstone family was unloading a quantity of second-rate or badly damaged furniture and other bric-a-brac—old leather suitcases, riding boots, towel rails, picnic baskets—the kind of thing that never would be eligible for the great London auction rooms of Christie's or Sotheby's but were likely to sell like hotcakes under a marquee on the grounds of a grand old place like Fasque. Bargain-hunting locals, travelers, and antiques dealers in dogged search of fresh material would gather like moths to a flame. To fill out the Fasque hoard, Bonham's was looking for similar stuff from other houses nearby.

Over the years there had been the odd dealer around to look at things. There was, for instance, the young Englishman who was interested in old luggage, strictly prewar. He was in the market of supplying movie-set designers and department- store window dressers with leather suitcases from the attics of old houses like the

Guynd. The young man himself—I've forgotten his name but I do remember his broad shoulders and shock of blond hair—was right out of *Chariots of Fire*. The cook's room yielded two or three items that matched his exacting standards, he wrote us a check, and off he went with them, crossing the Guynd off his list.

An antiquarian book dealer from Edinburgh named Ramsay phoned up from time to time. "Tell him I'm not here," John would say, squeezed in the vice between needing the cash and the pang of parting with a piece of the old library. Ramsay, who had spent an entire day combing the library, brushing past the cobwebs with an experienced hand, blowing the dust off the books, reaching past the front row of books into the back, knew exactly what we had. On the phone he would tell me that he had a client interested in *The Illustrated London News* or Humphrey Repton's *Pleasure Parks and Gardens*. Would Mr. Ouchterlony be willing to part with these?

"Tell him I'll have to think about it," said John when Ramsay called again. Did he really know what they were worth?

In a surprising change of tack from his usual caution, John did not strongly object when I suggested that we invite Bonham's over to inspect our inventory. We reviewed the material beforehand; there was nothing John would miss. If the sale brought in some cash, wonderful. If it didn't, it wouldn't be his fault. So along came Mark, an attractive young Englishman (*Chariots of Fire* again) in a suit, to view what we might have to offer.

In the dining room I had assembled some bits and pieces gathered from all over the house—wobbly side chairs, old curtains, tennis racquets, golf clubs, a pile of mismatched crystal prisms, a top hat in its fitted leather traveling case. "Right. Very salable," said Mark brightly, taking notes, cracking on. With rising confidence I led him deeper into the house. We squeezed past some old mattresses in the wine cellar to view a brass tea urn, "very good, Regency"—and a plain mahogany commode— "Right. George the Third." Then on upstairs to view a chest of drawers, "yup, Victorian. That'll do fine," and a *cheval* mirror. "These do very well." Then down to the farm buildings to uncover the old perambulators, circa 1900, a pair of Edwardian stained-glass panels, a partner's desk, and a pair of rusty wrought-iron plant stands.

"Should we spray paint them white?" I asked.

"No, no!" answered Mark without hesitation. "Just as they are, they'll do very well. You see," he added more thoughtfully, "people want to know that they're buying something really fresh on the market, that hasn't *been around*, if you see what I mean."

He spoke with that perfect combination of kindly and cunning. On the one hand he possessed that gentlemanly manner the auction man must cultivate in order to get away with the rather sensitive task of snooping through the back rooms of old family houses, handling the heirlooms in what might appear to be an impudent or overly familiar way, turning them upside down, pulling open drawers, checking them for breaks and scratches. On the other hand, he had that wink and nod that go with the tricks of the trade, of coaxing the two sides—buyer and seller—to let go of either their goods or their money, and convincing them both, as they walked away, that they had done extremely well. As Mark and I made our rounds John would calmly pop up here or there to check on our progress, or add a word, "That's a fine piece, solid cherry, mind you. My mother bought it for twenty quid," while also making it clear that he was in the midst of the more urgent chores of the day.

On the great day the marquee at Fasque was packed with collectors, dealers, and curiosity seekers from near and far. Ridiculous sums were bid for mere trifles—a collection of lamp stands needing paint and wiring, decrepit armchairs with the stuffing falling out, oil paintings filthy beyond all recognition. But the crowd had dwindled and the tent had begun to empty before our lots came up toward the end of the long afternoon. I bit my nails in the back row; John was quiet and cool beside me. As it turned out, though the show may have been over, the serious buyers were still in their seats and Bonham's, true to its word, sold virtually everything, much of it soaring over the estimate. John hardly flinched as the various bits of his heritage left his hands and in their place the cash rolled in. And sure enough, as I expected, we did not for a moment thereafter suffer the absence of any of it.

EIGHT

The County

. . .

"AND HOW IS THE SUN AND AIR?"

We were at a windy outdoor concert with friends and a picnic on the grounds of Glamis (say *Gloms*) Castle, seat of the Earl of Strathmore and childhood home of the Queen Mother. It was intermission and the audience of five hundred or so was in motion, stretching their legs, buying drinks in the tent, or parading around looking for people they knew. I was being greeted by a tall, over-weight gentleman with a florid complexion dressed in bright yellow and green summer tweed.

"The sun is great!" I replied, looking warily at a dark-ening cloud above us. "When it stays with us!" I added. I was trying to think of something witty to say about the air when I realized a beat later that my interlocutor was refer-ring not to the weather at all but to my son, the heir.

Nothing did Elliot yet know of heirdom, and that already his role was cast, that his family was not an entire-ly private matter but one that the surrounding community also considered its personal business. The Guynd had an heir, and I could tell that everyone who knew John's family had nearly lost hope of it ever happening.

It seemed that wherever we stepped out in Angus County society somebody had known John "since the year dot," or at school, or remembered him from dances, but hadn't seen him "for yonks!" Someone had been a good friend of his mother, another went shooting with his father, still another had been at school with his brother. "How's Angus?" they might ask. "Still in Canada?" Occasionally somebody thought John actually was his brother, as in "back from Canada now, are you?" Or perhaps they didn't know any of them at all but remembered swimming in their pool in the sixties. "And how's the Guynd?" was the constant refrain. It's like asking after the children.

You are the same as your house, or at least the house you came from, whether or not you still live in it. The intricacies, the innuendoes, piled higher the deeper I looked into just what that meant. Sometimes the house is named after the family; just as often the family is named after the house. It's not always clear which came first— the house name or the family name—or what's going to happen next. There are a lot of double-barreled names due to the bride's reluctance to give up her name entirely for the groom's, especially if hers is for some reason more distinguished, or if she is the last in the line, or if the house itself was demolished back in the 1920s. The Bowes Lyons, the Bruce Gardynes, the MacMillan Douglases, the Blair Imries, the Campbell Adamsons, the Carnegie Arbuthnots are just a few that have resulted from this tenacity to family names in Angus.

There are also hidden subtleties to be known about the more commonplace names such as Grant. At a cocktail party I was introduced to a petite, fair-haired young lady, a somebody-or-other Grant from Aberdeenshire; another guest beside me knew enough to press, "Are you a Grant of Glenmoriston?" "No," she replied without a blink, "of Moneymusk," and whatever understanding passed thus between the two of them as to what being from one or the other branch implied as to their character, wealth, depth of history, or eccentricity was entirely lost on me. But I could tell by the knowing of their expressions that Miss Grant had just imparted a volume of information in her two simple words, "of Moneymusk."

"I don't like Scotland," Princess Di told a news reporter in one of her candid moods. She regularly endured the required month at the royal retreat of Balmoral, unhappily appearing at the grouse shoot or salmon run with her tartan shawl and picnic basket. It wasn't so much that she didn't enjoy the outdoor life, which was so much a part of her own background at Althorp. "It's the people in the large houses I don't like," she explained. No doubt she found it no haven from the social pressures of the south. For in spite of its relative poverty, in spite of its tiny population of five million, Scotland is studded with dukes and marquesses, earls and viscounts. There is more nobility per square mile of Scotland than anywhere else in the UK. And their tenacity to land and title is unsurpassed.

Life in this society, I decided, was simply one of passing through the familial territory until it is finally your turn to join the ghosts and get on with what really matters: haunting the living with the ever-lengthening shadows of the past.

Even the newcomers to Angus, the young families—the English, the Anglo-Irish—quickly catch on to the point. At a birthday party for four-year-old Alexander I met a young mother of three boys, newcomers from England. Sassy, a peppy, dark-eyed beauty, immediately asked me where we lived. "Carmyllie," I answered, then adding, "about five miles east of Arbroath." Pressing further, Sassy asked me if our house had a name. "The Guynd!" she exclaimed. "I've always wondered where that was. You're right next to our house in *Forfarshire Illustrated!*"

Assuming that I would know what she was talking about, and fortunately I did, as we had a copy in our own library, Sassy was referring to a book of engravings illustrating all the notable houses and castles in Angus circa 1860, when the county was called Forfarshire. Sassy and her husband had recently bought a house called Ardovie near the town of Brechin. Not one to miss a beat she was on the phone a few days later asking me and Elliot over for lunch. Ardovie was as sweet as its name, a secluded high plain with a panoramic view of the countryside, and inside it was all flowers and stripes and scented with homegrown lavender. In her Aga-warmed kitchen Sassy turned out a comforting roast and a velvety pudding. Not long after that I returned the invitation to the Guynd for tea and a walk, and thus the longtime neighbors on the pages of *Forfarshire Illustrated* became friends. From then on, if Sassy was introducing me to someone she would immediately add, "Do you know the Guynd? *Gorgeous* house," as if to assure them that despite the American accent I was, you know, an insider.

Though I often felt less like an insider than a voyeur, I was beginning to learn how to hold up my end of a dinner party conversation in Angus, or at least what sort of questions to ask. I might ask with growing interest about who was opening her garden this year in aid of what, or whether or not Mrs. So-and-So's house—a fine house but not exactly world class—deserved its new A-listed status, and what good it would do her anyway. I was becoming haltingly conversant on the economic implications of the proposed ban on fox hunting, or the problems for landowners posed by the ramblers' "right to roam." And what about these "new age travelers" who arrived en masse at country estates and then refused to leave as some sort of social protest? And were we in favor of *devolution,* or was it just going to create more busy bureaucrats who hadn't a clue about the issues of the countryside? I could talk pheasants, if I had to, I could talk Dysons.

Scottish history, especially as it relates to family history, was a surefire topic, especially with the gents. Somebody's American houseguest seated next to me at a dinner party said that he'd heard that in Scotland the social evening would not be over before someone mentioned "the '45". He was referring of course to the Rebellion of 1745 led by Bonnie Prince Charlie, which they still talk about in Scotland as if it happened yesterday. They argue over whether or not Bonnie Prince Charlie, sometimes called "the Young Pretender," and brutally crushed at the Battle of Culloden, was a tragic hero or a vainglorious fool. They love to discuss—if they don't know for certain—who among their own ancestry were his fellow Jacobites. Highlanders, romantics, and Catholics, I found, tend to relate themselves to Charlie; Lowlanders, Protestants, and more practical characters tend to side with the Loyalists. It was after this uprising that many Jacobites fled the country (including most of the Ouchterlonys), and the English banished every symbol of Scottish culture and tradition—the kilts, the bagpipes, the works. For seventy years the Scots endured being stripped of their identity, until George IV fell in love with Scotland and awarded knighthood to Sir Walter Scott, his neice Queen Victoria took on Balmoral, and between them they brought it all back into fashion. Nevertheless the matter has not yet been put to rest in the Scottish mind, and the interest in the figure of the Bonnie Prince and the crushing blow to their country that he symbolized is apparently inexhaustible. Sure enough down the dinner table someone—in fact it was John—was nattering on about how his third cousin six times removed did not flee after the '45; indeed, he was officially protected by the crown because he had written the first statistical account of the county and was therefore terribly useful et cetera et cetera. "You see, it's happened," I said to my dinner partner. "Now you can relax."

I needed a godmother, so far away as I was from home, the guiding hand of older feminine wisdom. Tess was such a lady. She immediately took me under her wing, as she had been a close friend of John's mother; they had shared much, and she knew the family intimately. Still beautiful in her sixties, elegant and poised, though she walked with a cane as a result of a car accident, Tess was no stranger to tragedy, nor to privilege. Her weariness and bright cheerfulness were an inexorable combination that made her a touching friend from the start. "Poor John, his father was very hard on him," she told me in her quick, high little voice. "Of course he was hard on Doreen too. I'm sure you've heard . . ."

"They more or less led separate lives, didn't they?" I asked, begging for more from that store of intimate family knowledge Tess possessed, groping for the next leading question. "Did they share any friends at all?"

"Not really. You see everything, including friendships, became a sort of competition between them. But especially the boys, especially the boys. He was especially hard on John. Angus, being the younger one, was a bit more coddled."

Being the second son was hard enough, I had thought. Being first was worse.

"And of course you've heard about Tom's *condition*," she went on, very quietly now, as if someone might be about to enter the room.

"Well, I know that——"

"Depression. Mood swings. They say he never recovered from being a prisoner of war in Germany."

"What *did* happen? I thought he was supposed to have been relatively comfortable," I ventured.

"My dear, nobody knows."

Without exactly telling me what to do, Tess took a great interest in the look of the house and the changes we were making. Concealing as best she could her own strong taste, she congratulated me on every change I made, knowing that with every step change itself had been my greatest challenge, as it had also been for Doreen. In Tess's mind this was my role, to carry on for Doreen's sake, to realize what she hadn't been able to. "I think that's very good," said Tess, viewing two solid weeks worth of my work on the stone staircase, stripping several coats of painted faux effects over the course of at least a hundred years. (John had hounded my progress practically every step of the way with an ongoing barrage of blistering criticism of my work methods, as if scraping toxic chemicals wasn't enough of a punishment. In spite of the obstacles I got it done.) "Doreen would be so pleased," said Tess. Casting her critical eye around, she then added brightly, "Now all you have to do is polish the brass carpet rails!"

Tess never criticized what was already said and done, but if a decorating decision was still to be made she would offer her frank opinion. "I wouldn't call that a pretty fabric," she said, inspecting a piece of Indian print linen with one of those bold, sinuous floral patterns, in fact an old curtain I had pulled out of the cellar. "And it *is* a pretty chair. It should have a pretty fabric. Do you see what I mean?" I did, actually. It was just that I thought she might be impressed with my effort to recycle the old materials. Wouldn't that have pleased Doreen?

I confided in Tess the details of our battle over what color to paint the dining room. John was for something called "Hot Sahara," and I, at the other end of the spectrum, preferred "Deep Worcester Blue." Tess did not hesitate to contribute her opinion to the debate. "Blue is rather unusual for a dining room," she admitted, on John's side, "because blue is cold. But," she went on, as I held up the swatch for her inspection, "this velvety dark blue you have in mind, in a room this size, with your white wainscoting and pillars, and your note of scarlet in the chair seats— these are gorgeous! Did you make these little slipcovers?"

"Well, I had them made . . ."

"And I'm glad to see that you haven't pulled up the original horsehair underneath, that would have been a great mistake. But anyway, you've asked me about the blue. With the warmth of your furniture, the blue might be extremely elegant." Then, as a little tip of the day, Tess informed me that the wine cooler, a standard piece of country house equipment—oval, tin-lined, brass-buckled, four-legged oak—belonged under the sideboard. At her insistence we tried it on the spot and she was, as usual, so right.

Every so often Tess could not resist reminding me that I was an American, a city girl, and how was I to know.

Like when I planted a dark red rhododendron by the old swimming pool without putting bonemeal in the hole first. "Oh, that was very naughty," she told me. I tried to defend my carelessness by pointing out that rhododendrons grew like weeds in Scotland, didn't they? "Oh but you see they were planted in the days when they had gardeners, and they knew what to do to make the roots take hold." I rushed out to the nearest garden center for bonemeal, and luckily I was able to lift the plant easily, pour in a little of the magic white powder, and pop it down again.

Tess had deep gossip, not just who was who and who their parents were and what their children were doing, but whether or not they had done their bit for the county, what personal tragedies had shaped them, where the children had gone wrong and why. Tess was also a networker par excellence, and she was anxious for me to connect with other women who had children the same age as Elliot, or who shared my interest in art. For instance, she steered me toward an event organized by an art-minded American lady named Ann, who with her English husband had recently moved up from Hampshire and bought a Victorian castle called Lundie. Tess offered me an invitation to a lecture at Lundie in aid of a foundation that funded eye care in developing countries, with a buffet lunch afterward. Ann had invited a curator up from the Tate Gallery in London to lecture on "the swagger portrait."

The hall of the castle was packed with ladies on folding chairs. As Ann stood up to welcome us, I felt immediately proud of my fellow American. She was the very picture of the charity lady—tall, elegant, smiling, a touch of the debutante about her, even in her fifties—and the speaker she had persuaded to come way up north was erudite and amusing, devoting a considerable amount of time to native Scots like Ramsay and Raeburn. Lunch was cold poached salmon and salad and a glass of South African chardonnay. When finally the ladies got into their little cars and drove off down the tree-lined drive, they appeared highly satisfied with the break in their country routine.

Ann was quick to solicit my membership to another of her favorite charities, the National Art Collections Fund, which for the past hundred years has been raising money to keep works of art from being sold abroad, often to rich Americans. Though I felt slightly torn in my loyalties between the preservation of the old world and the education of the new, an undeniably attractive feature of membership to the NACF in the far-flung provinces was the opportunity to go on members' tours to interesting houses and collections otherwise closed to the public.

My first NACF trip was to Balcarres (Bal-*car*-ees), the castle home of Lord Crawford of the ancient Lindsay clan. A busload of about thirty of us, mostly ladies, were hurtled one hour south into Fife to be shown through the castle by the Lord himself and the Lady. We admired their Gainsborough portraits, Renaissance panel paintings, Fortuny fabric wall covering, and brocade curtains from the sale of Marie Antoinette's personal effects, and after a cup of tea we toured the garden and grounds. Balcarres is situated on a hill with a wide-open view of the North Sea and the famous Bass Rock, rising like a giant's knee out of the deep.

"What a spectacular view!" I exclaimed to Lord Crawford as we passed through the garden gate onto the lawn. He offered me a seat on a garden chair nearby, and sat down beside me, explaining that the Bass Rock was one of a drift of volcanic deposits left over from the ice age. I asked him if the ivy on the castle helped to insulate it from the damp, and was it true that the Scots believed that ivy kept the witches away, by which time he had detected that I was American.

"My son lives there," he admitted. "Do you know Connecticut? They live in a town called Greenwich," and adding a little doubtfully that "they seem to be quite happy there."

"Oh Greenwich is very attractive," I assured him.

"Yes I know it is," replied Lord Crawford. "All the same, it seems a rather competitive atmosphere to me, full of rather large houses." As he gazed out over his unspoiled view of the sea without another building in sight, he added, "Rather close together."

Before long Ann was suggesting, in her winning way, that I might join her committee of Angus ladies and that, furthermore, we might offer the Guynd as a venue for an NACF luncheon. How could I refuse, especially as it appeared to make the perfect case for getting the dining room painted at last?

John rose to the occasion, and he even agreed to my choice of Deep Worcester Blue. The paint was expensive, to be sure. And it had to be shipped from John Oliver, a decorator's shop in London. "Can't we just go down to the DIY in Dundee and have the color matched?" asked John. But I argued that, as Patrick would say, quality paint is like strong coffee. They don't make it like that in Dundee.

On the big day about forty members showed up, their hunger keen after a tour of a private castle nearby, and the cold buffet was laid on by my fellow committee members who cheerfully navigated their way around the construction site that we called our kitchen. Over pudding, I was pressed into giving a brief history of the house and the family—how the Ouchterlonys had settled at the Guynd four hundred years ago, how the mansion house and the park conformed to the Regency ideal, and so on, and so forth, I went on and on, into the eerie silence of a roomful of polite tourists. You could have heard a pin drop.

"I knew your husband *ages* ago," said one of the ladies afterward. About John's vintage, I reckoned. "Is he here?"

To be sure he was somewhere. But having left the speechmaking to me, in the end he dodged the entire affair.

"I'm afraid there was something he urgently had to deal with at the farm buildings," I invented on the spot. "How do you like the wall color? John just finished painting the day before yesterday!"

"Well done," said Tess, giving me a pat on the back, as the last few cars rolled away down the drive. "The dining room is a triumph. Now if you could only do something about that kitchen . . ."

Clearly, heritage organizations were the way of the country. I persuaded John that, having joined the NACF, we should also become members of the HHA. The Historic Houses Association was formed in response to the creeping demise of country houses and parks. There was a need for solidarity, for the far-flung owners of stately piles all over Britain to unite against the shifting tides of labor politics, farming methods, building restrictions, conservation grants, tax relief, tenantry, country sports, winter storms, and dry rot. After the wars the HHA emerged as a lobby group for an endangered species. By now an established institution, the HHA membership looks forward to its regular bulletins from the latest battlefront, its quarterly magazine, and especially the annual meeting. Every July, the Scottish branch of the HHA holds its own AGM at the house of one of its members, with lunch and house tour afterward, making it a real day out. In spite of the group having formed around the problems of country house ownership, in spite of the business at hand being deadly serious, I found that the annual meeting was a festive and highly social affair. Country house ownership, from the look of this event, was not all bad news.

All it takes to become a member of the HHA is your title to a historic house and your annual membership dues. However, the range of wealth and importance among these 250 Scottish houses is considerable, from famous historic landmarks open to the public such as Glamis at the top end to small country estates like the Guynd at the other. When the problems of tourism and film-location deals and whether or not to lend the Poussin came up for discussion, I felt we were somewhat out of our depth. But there was always the chance that we would learn something useful.

One year the Scottish branch met at Dalmeny House, near Edinburgh, home of the Earl and Countess of Roseberry. As we approached the Gothic Revival mansion rising from a spacious lawn with a magnificent view of the Firth of Forth, I reviewed the list of members. I was learning to wrap my mouth around names like Drumlanrig, that the Duke of Buccleuch was pronounced Ba*clue*, to remember that the "z" in Culzean (Cul-*lane*) is silent, and that Newe rhymes with "meow."

We were greeted at Dalmeny in the front hall, two stories high with a wide staircase rising through it, and offered morning coffee and shortbread. As the hall became crammed with members I searched the crowd for familiar faces, finding very few. Sassy introduced me to a tall, middle-aged man with a stack of titles, Lord Something of Such and Such, as well as Lord Something of Somewhere else, and as he vigorously shook my hand amid the jostling of guests moving in, he tipped my cup of black coffee onto the front of my brand-new ice-green Laura Ashley jacket right on down to my floral print trousers. The lord's mouth fell open and so did mine. As he sputtered profuse apologies, I turned to one of the waitresses serving coffee, who immediately rushed me upstairs to a bedroom with a washbasin. I instantly shed my garments and started filling the basin with water. "Cold water or hot, do you think?" I asked.

"Cold!" she cried and hurried out of the room.

A moment later our hostess, Lady Roseberry, appeared. "How do you do?" I said, extending my hand, trying to remember my best manners as I stood before her Ladyship in my underwear. "I'm Mrs. Ouchterlony." The unflappable countess quickly sized up my figure and dashed off to look for something suitable for me to wear from her own wardrobe.

I reappeared in time for the formal part of the meeting, dressed in Lady Roseberry's white blouse and blue skirt, and my own clothes in a plastic bag ("Keep them damp." instructed the waitress firmly), as the chairman began his report. "My lords, ladies, and gentlemen," he began his charming opening words, before sliding inevitably into the technical. "The EU has extended for another year dispensation under annex K . . . " while I found myself studying the lady's hat in front of me and wondering what was for lunch.

Lunch was quiche lorraine and potato salad, followed by raspberry "pavlova" *and* chocolate bread pudding (the Scots adore their "pudding," of which there are always at least two at a social occasion, and with very little effort they can be persuaded to have both). I sat next to a large, elderly woman called the Lady Strange, who I learned was the last of the Drummonds. Her husband, Lord Drummond, on my other side, had given up the name of his Welsh ancestors (Evans) for hers. They lived in her family pile in Perthshire called Megginch, famous among other things for its tipsy-looking topiary and a large collection of stuffed birds. It also became evident that the Drummonds had a way with dogs, as soon they were all around our table and under it, the Lady slipping pieces of quiche to the retriever on my right, the Lord his Stilton cheese to the spaniel on my left. I confessed that at the Guynd we let the dogs lick the dinner plates (and did I dare to add that the dogs were admonished for *not* licking the plates properly?). "Very sanitizing," agreed the Lady Strange.

The Earl and Countess of Southesk, our neighbors in Angus, were also at the meeting. This attractive young couple was among those Tess had recommended to me with children the same age as Elliot, whom I should get to know. Though they were known as the Southesks, after a river, their family name was actually Carnegie (the Scots say Car-*nay*-gie, not *Car*negie) and they lived in a castle called Kinnaird.

"When are you supposed to call them Car*nay*gie and when Southesk?" I asked John.

"I haven't any idea," he answered. "But *you* can ask!"

I asked Isobel Strathmore, of Glamis, instead. Their situation is even more complicated. Isobel and her husband are the Earl and Countess of Strathmore and Kinghorne, but their children are the Bowes Lyons, except for the eldest son, who is Lord Glamis, until he becomes the Earl of Strathmore. His siblings, however, will always be Bowes Lyons. It's simple, really.

Before long, the Countess of Southesk was just Caroline to me, thank goodness. An energetic blonde with a petite frame but powerful voice that develops in women who raise small boys in large houses, she had what seemed to me a total and unpretentious confidence in how to play the role she had married into. David had inherited the castle at the tender age of twenty-nine, due to the fact that the Carnegie family had so many other titles and other castles to deal with. But for so young a couple the obligations to the title were great. For they represented Angus nobility, and Caroline knew that with the title came its duties to the crown; her eldest son, for instance, would be expected to perform as a page at the queen's jubilee. And as clan chief David would have to show up in Canada from time to time to be hailed by scores of Canadian Carnegies and to lead them in Scottish jigs and reels.

While raising three boys, Caroline had whipped the castle into shape—repainted the walls, recovered the chairs, restored the pictures—and at the same time made Kinnaird the host of charity and community events all year-round. They opened the grounds to Riding for the Disabled, and the castle halls for an embroidery exhibition in aid of Save the Children, dinners and lectures in aid of the NACF. In the game room Caroline hosted a children's play group three days a week, and—to help her unwind from her hectic life—a weekly yoga class. I became a regular at this last offering.

Every Tuesday morning anywhere from three to eight young mothers (at least ten years younger than me) gathered in the game room at the back of the castle, rolled out our mats on the polished wooden floor, and settled down for some serious relaxation. Our instructor, a short, plump, middle-aged Dundonian named Maggie, told us to forget our worries, forget our husbands, our children—everything, she said with a rolling *r*, but "yerselves," and especially any negative feelings we might be fostering inside. "Say good-bye," she would tell us firmly. "Let them go." Once assured that we had sufficiently drained our minds of our cares she started the stretching exercises. Finally, toward the end of the ninety-minute session, we lay on our backs for the last relaxation exercise, with Maggie hypnotizing us with her soothing words and wind-chimey taped music. Then my stretched muscles would melt into the floor and my mind would open up to buried longings—such as a really hot summer day, followed by a warm, breezy evening in which I might be sitting on a porch somewhere in seaside New England. I would leave the rows of antlers and tartan curtains, the stormy Scottish sky outside the window, and drift away home.

SEPTEMBER COMES AND with it the County Ball. In Angus this is a Highland dance, as the Angus Glens are among the foothills of the Highlands. Gents are expected to dress in kilts of their family tartan, with black tie, boiled shirt, black waist-length jacket, and hairy sporran. Shoes are shiny black and buckled, and socks are colored to more or less match the kilt (*never* white at the ball, that would be "frightfully pipe-bandish," Alison explained to me), with a stout red ribbon to secure them just below the knee. The ladies dress in their finest taffeta ball gowns, with plenty of skirt to swirl around in, and a tartan sash ("over the left shoulder, always," advised Alison, "and you'll need a brooch to keep it in place.")

As a boy John had been sent off to join other upper-class children to practice their Highland dances in the basement of someone's castle, until they knew the stuff cold. Later in life, said Alison, if you're rusty, or have a partner from south of the border, you might organize a practice dance or, failing that, you can brush up at home with a tape player and a line of pillows.

Unfortunately John had enough faith in my native talent to think that I would just catch on, and I, having been to a few American square dances in my time, thought so too. As it turned out, when I found myself in a huge marquee attached to Glamis Castle at my first Angus County Ball, it was a little more complicated than that. Actually, these jigs and reels are very intricate, fast-paced, and full of contrapuntal twists and shifts of partner. Furthermore, such a formal occasion never includes a "caller" shouting instructions over the blare of the band, as they do in America. While the point of an American folk dance is to bring everyone onto the same level, the point of the ball in Scotland is to divide those who know the complicated dances, such as "Hamilton House," "The Broun's Reel", and "The Duke and Duchess of Edinburgh" (the upper classes) from those who know only the rowdier ones like "Strip the Willow" (the lower), who aren't invited anyway.

Our group consisted of old friends of John's who had danced together since childhood. The evening began with a dinner party at a Victorian castle, Kinblethmont, family home of the Ramsays. Robert, with his flared nostrils and long bony face ending in a neatly groomed goatee, could have stepped right out of one of those swagger portraits. Men look great in kilts, I decided, especially Scottish men. And Penny's dinner was so sumptuous and leisurely that the evening, as far as I was concerned, could have easily ended right there. But then the little dance cards were distributed around the table, with their pencils dangling from a silken cord, and "Can I have you for the 'Dashing White Sergeant'?" asked Robert and someone else put me down for the "Eightsome Reel," and I could tell we were in for a long evening.

When we finally arrived at the ball, it was getting on toward eleven. We claimed our table and leapt into the fray. John's friends were very forgiving as my head spun, my eyes searched for signals, my hands for other hands— or was it the elbow this time—and my feet simply had to follow along. John's firm hand met me here and there, his arm encircled my waist, and from across the set he shouted encouragement, "That's it! On you go!" or frantic instructions, "The guy to your left, *to your left!*"

To the swish of brightly colored taffeta, the twirl of heavy tartan kilts, and the glint of silver buckles, the dance went on and on, four hundred strong. Breakfast of eggs and bacon was served in the old vaulted kitchen of the castle. The hour was way past midnight, in fact it was nearly three A.M., and no one was even thinking of leaving.

For the Scots have an altogether different sense of time. Is it because there are days in summer that go on so long you think they'll never end, and then days in winter that don't deserve to be called days at all? Is it because they travel such long, lonely distances over the countryside to gather together that, once arrived, they hate to go? In the old days an evening party depended on a clear night and a full moon for the guests to travel the rough roads in horse-drawn carriages. And the annual ball was effectively a clan meeting, lasting several days. An orgy of merriment, it is the last gasp of summer before the winter sets in with its interminable nights. The Scots feel more intensely than most people the difference between company and solitude, lightness and dark.

I blended into the crowd, caught up in the music, swinging from partner to partner. A sea of faces flashed by, and none of them had any idea where I had come from. My friends back home, meanwhile, had no idea where I was. Could they picture me now, in the midst of this tent full of rollicking, reeling Highlanders? I was suspended in time, going through my paces, following directions, as if in a play.

Part Three

NINE

Play Piece

. . .

MORE THAN THE ANGUS BALL, OR THE NACF, OR the HHA, more than anybody or anything, it was Elliot who was my main entree into Angus society. County society is built from the ground up, and solidarity begins at a young age. The heir to the Guynd was supposed to mix with other heirs to other estates. It went without saying that these children would likely be mixing for decades to come, attending the same parties and dances, meeting in exactly the same houses and, as they grew older, comparing their problems over the latest farming methods or the damage from last winter's storms.

As far as I was concerned, the immediate point was that Elliot needed playmates. By the time he was four or five I was in search of an ever wider range of friends for him, even if it meant driving half an hour or more to some other corner of the county to meet them. I discovered that the county of Angus—if you knew where to look for them—was swarming with little boys. As mothers of small children are driven to congregate and support one another, our circles thus naturally widened, with a birthday party at Kinnaird castle followed up by an invitation to lunch at Glamis or a game of football at Airlie. The settings for such gatherings were enchanting in the first place, but to see children at play on those emerald lawns made them all the more so. At times, I was certain we were giving Elliot an idyllic childhood, at times it was what any American would have called a fairy tale.

At other times I wasn't so sure. Elliot was an only child. He was shy and sensitive to crowds. But these other children seemed to move everywhere in packs; they invaded one another's houses en masse, they ate bangers and beans at long, noisy tables, they freely used and abused each other's toys. They disbursed into smaller groups and created little wars among themselves, playing swords with sticks, taking refuge in tree houses. Elliot entered the fray gingerly, if indeed he did not altogether refuse to get out of the car.

John was less dismayed by Elliot's shyness than by his lack of manners. Frequently, these were related issues. Like the time we were all invited to a formal Sunday lunch for about twenty people at Blair Adam. All the children were seated together at the far end of the dining room table, all of them strangers to Elliot. Almost at once, at a loss for anything better to do including eating his dinner, Elliot slipped under the table. I watched the other children obediently, wordlessly eating, using their knives and forks properly, saying "yes please" and "no thank you" to whatever was offered them, good as gold. And then the anxious exchange of glances among them, some giggles, a frown. I poked my head under the table and discovered Elliot quietly untying everybody's shoes.

At the same time as mixing with the gentry, it was important to us that Elliot get to know our nearest neighbors. He had to learn the dialect—if not to speak it, at least to understand it—and this he would never learn from the children of our friends with their proper English accents. We signed him up for the local primary school in Carmyllie, about two miles up the road from the front gate of the Guynd. There he would mix with the children of the local farmers, the car mechanic, the joiner, and the disabled and unemployed who lived in the council houses in the village. Thus Elliot would provide an entree into another aspect of Angus society.

The Scots are rightly proud of their school system. Ever since John Knox declared his determination to rebuild Jerusalem on the rubble heap of papist Britain, education has been given a high priority. In sixteenth-century Scotland, rural communities formed around the parish church, or *kirk*, and it was determined that "the heritors of every parish should provide a commodious house for a school." It was essential, in Knox's opinion, that every Scottish boy and girl, every man and woman, learn to read the Bible. Knox's vision was carried out with such remarkable success that travelers in sixteenth-century Scotland were astonished at the literacy—the actual love of books and learning—displayed among a population whose living conditions were in other ways as primitive as those of tribal Africa.

A sense of democracy was instilled early in the life of the Scot. For every level of society converged in the local schoolhouse where "the laird's and the ploughman's son, the sons of the carpenter and the lord of session, met together." Later, around the age of eight, in order to learn his Latin, the laird's son was sent to a school in the nearest burgh, which was inevitably too far from home for a daily commute, so he would pay for his room and board. Thus the tradition of boarding school became as deeply ingrained in the Scottish psyche as anywhere else in Britain, a system that persists to this day, serving to colonize the children of the countryside where private day schools are few and far between.

For the time being, our plan for Elliot's later years remained in the air. Sending a child away to school at the age of eight was to me a daunting prospect. I thought of Roald Dahl's accounts of his early years at boarding school—of menacing prefects and sadistic matrons—though that was some time ago; things were supposed to be more humane nowadays. "He's going to love it," said Sassy firmly about the prospect of sending her eldest off to Belhaven. "It's going to be so good for him." Whether they themselves had loved or hated it, the upper-class British parent tends to regard boarding school as something that simply has to be endured. "They come home almost every weekend," Sassy assured me, "and parents show up at the games all the time."

Both of the boarding schools John attended had closed—the first, a small Catholic prep school in the Borders, the second, a monastic fortress on the south shore of Loch Ness—so we were liberated from that legacy at least. I'd seen John's letters to his mother from school, saying what he was meant to say, the homesick boy keeping a stiff upper lip, while the master hovered over him. These letters were as carefully censored as his father's from wartime Germany. "We have had a great deal of rain this week, on two days we had half an inch and on others a bit less," wrote John from the Carlekamp Priory School in North Berwick, aged eleven. "It was only a small boil on my knee, got two more but that's not much," reported Angus, aged nine. "One day at tea we had sandwich spread."

I wondered if that famous British sense of irony that John took such pride in might have something to do with the heartbreak of leaving home at the tender age of eight. They learned to compensate, to disguise their true longings, their little aches and pains; they learned to play them down. Wrenched from his mother's embrace at that age, does the man he becomes still seek the gentle transition into adolescence he was never given the time to make? Is he forever after looking for that mother love, though his instinct to ask for it has been snapped in the bud?

With the question of boarding school tabled for the time being, we prepared Elliot for Carmyllie School. A few days before the school opened for the autumn term its administrators issued their instructions. A hot lunch would be provided for a pound, and in addition each child was asked to bring somthing they call a "play piece," which means a snack for morning recess. This typically consists of a bag of crisps (potato chips) and a Mars Bar and something equally sweet and sticky to drink. And if you put an apple or a carrot in there, it will be ignored. Elliot was offered a uniform—red sweatshirt, gray trousers—which he calmly refused to wear. In fact it was not a requirement, even though all the other children wore them. I only hoped that he wouldn't feel too out of step with his classmates, with already so much to set him apart—his big estate, his American accent. But this did not seem to concern five-year-old Elliot, whose innately independent character was already asserting itself. He was shy but, once over his shyness, determinably unconventional.

The old stone schoolhouse stands by the side of the road; behind it a field of wheat spreads out to the horizon. At nine o'clock the yellow school bus unloads and a few cars come and go. A child takes hold of the rope at the bottom of the bell tower, pulls hard, and loudly clangs the start of the school day. Though it looked as grim as a workhouse from the outside, I was relieved to find that Primary One, Two, and Three shared a bright, cheerful room in the modern addition. The experienced Mrs. Jeans presided over her fifteen students who altogether constituted her three grades. She set each group in motion with their workbooks and then moved on to the next.

At first I wondered if Elliot was following everything

that was going on, if he even understood what the teacher was saying. No, he didn't, he admitted matter-of-factly. His beginning attempts at phonetic reading became doubly challenging when a long o, as in "snow," was pronounced "snoo," and a long *a* as in "bay" was pronounced "bee." But within a few weeks of starting Carmyllie School he understood the local accent better than I did, and was employing enough of it to make himself understood—trilling his *r*'s, softening his *o*'s, and adding a distinctly Scottish lilt just before a question mark. I noticed certain native turns of phrase such as that he would be doing something not "on" but "at" the weekend, he would say that his toy "needed fixed," skipping the "to be," and when he was finished with a task he would announce "that's me done" or, simply, "that's me."

At recess Elliot held his own in discussions of farm machinery; he knew just as much about the workings of a tractor, a sprayer, or a potato harvester as any of the other little boys. Between his familiarity with the farm, the novelty of his American accent, and his impish appearance, Elliot was regarded with some interest by his classmates. "He's very popular," Mrs. Jeans assured me. "Everybody likes him."

Yet in this little village of Carmyllie, where many of the inhabitants had never traveled farther than Dundee, Elliot was bound to be looked upon not only with interest but also with suspician and jealousy. He was different; he was an outsider, and he knew it. Somethimes this seemed to bother him and sometimes it didn't. "Hello Elliot!" a chorus of voices would greet him loud and clear as I walked him through the door of the school, to which he would raise a limp hand to wave and then roll his eyes skyward.

I was also concerned about what went on at so-called playtime. That's when the "play piece" comes out of the lunch box and the children are released from the classroom. If it was a wet day the children played in the hall; if it was dry they were sent out into the yard. The yard consisted of a bit of grass, a lot of tarmac, and a single Scots pine—perfect for climbing—which the children were not allowed to climb. There was a hedge along the south wall that the children liked to hide in, and so did the occasional sheep from the neighboring farm. There was a hole in a dead tree around the back where the boys stirred up mud and gravel with sticks. Other than that there was not a great deal to play with at playtime.

At one point the boys went through a phase of lifting the girls' skirts until they screamed with rage and stormed off to the office to tell on them. Then there was a trend for busting up their juice cartons, having only sucked in a strawful, the remains of the bright orange or purple liquid burst onto the tarmac. Once that trick had run its course they threw pinecones at passing cars. Occasionally Elliot came home with a bruise. "What happened here?" I would ask him. Eventually he would tell me. Scott and Ross were ganging up on him.

Scott and Ross were best friends. Scott's father was a farmhand. He worked for Webster who farmed several fields at the Guynd every year. Ross's father had his own fields. His family was as deeply rooted in the Angus countryside as John's was. But Ross's father wasn't a laird.

"Why isn't Ross's father a laird?" I asked John. "He's a landowner, so why isn't he a laird?"

He just wasn't. John couldn't explain it. Did one have to be born a laird? It helps, but it's not absolutely necessary. The title went with the property, not the man. As to a lot of straight questions one might ask in Scotland, there seemed to be no straight answer but rather something more complicated, like an impression built of many layers. You had to have stood your ground for several generations. You had to have tenants to be a laird. It implied that you had a rather grand house, which Ross's father did not have.

Yet the farmer had much to be proud of. He was the exemplary hardworking, respectable country man. His ancestors were those favored by the landowners in the days of the agricultural improvements. They were the ones who acquired a piece of their own, and formed the rural middle class. During the Second World War the farmers' skills and machinery were so highly valued they were given free petrol from the government. To be a farmer was to be somebody. To be a farmer's daughter, as I vividly recalled the example of Mrs. Sheret—with her needlework, her china teacups, and her perfectly coiffed hair—was to hold your head high. Yet it was clear that the farmer was not of the same class as the laird. I had a feeling this made Ross uncomfortable with Elliot. He had encountered, perhaps for the first time in his life, his more-than-equal, but it didn't square with him that the buildings at the Guynd seemed to be caving in, that Elliot's father looked like a hippie, and his mother was American.

John took these schoolboy rivalries as par for the course. "Elliot will learn to defend himself," he promised.

"Kids is kids, Belinda,'" our neighbor Davina reminded me, "especially boys."

I was nevertheless distressed that the children were sent out to play with no supervision except when it was called for, by which time it was a small crisis. At a PTA meeting I suggested to the assembled six or eight mothers and the head teacher, Mr. Taylor, that we might try to raise the funds for some playground equipment. It was no wonder the lads were out of hand; there was nothing for them to do, no props for their play. Couldn't we obtain a simple climbing frame, create a sandpit, and perhaps install a bench so that parents could congregate after school, bundle up against the wind, and watch the children play? Doubt and scorn were instantly poured upon this strange Yankee concept. The children would fall off the climbing frame and hurt themselves. Oh, aye. They would track sand into the building. You can be sure of that. Anyway it would be too expensive. Oh, aye.

Having been put squarely in my place by the PTA I could at least offer the Guynd as a recreational facility for the schoolchildren. I suggested they go bird-watching, or perhaps take a walk around the lake to study how a lake over the years becomes a bog. Discussing the prospects with Mrs. Jeans, she discerned a perfect venue for her annual "safety walk." The path to the temple was just right. Since Elliot's christening five years earlier it had become overgrown and blocked by fallen timber, and John's little palette bridges were rotting. So one October afternoon Primary One, Two, and Three rolled through the front gates of the Guynd in a couple of Land Rovers, down to the dip in the road where the path to the temple leads into the woods, and set off on their hazardous walk, leaping across fallen trees and navigating the "wee broken bridges." Everyone returned unscathed and now they could all say they had been to the Guynd.

It wasn't long before Elliot was invited to play at other children's houses. Stephanie, whose father was a mechanic, in fact he was our mechanic, was something of a tomboy. She and Elliot played in the sandpit with toy tractors and jumped around the piles of old cars that surrounded her father's garage. Visiting the Guynd Stephanie donned oversize Wellies out of the cloakroom and waded into the old pool with a butterfly net, fishing for water bugs. And she taught Elliot how to make a daisy chain. I couldn't get Stephanie to eat anything more than a fistful of chocolate Cheerios. On the other hand if she invited Elliot for "tea" at Fernlea, he would emerge with a full tummy and the telltale whiff of the deep-fryer about him.

Shirley Jayne, another classmate, came over to play one day after school. I picked her up at the kitchen door of her house where her plump, blond, smiling mother waved us off under a wooden sign carved with the words "Kids For Sale." Shirley Jayne was not so much of a tomboy, and not so interested in water bugs as Stephanie. Arriving at the Guynd her eyes eagerly roamed the front hall, checking everything. "Did posh people used to live here?" she ventured.

Seeing as John and I clearly did not make the grade as posh people in Shirley Jayne's estimation, I answered, "Yes, Elliot's ancestors were fairly posh people. They built this house."

Shirley Jayne wasn't done yet. She eyed the dining room sideways through the open door. Pointing, she asked, "Is that where you have yer tea?"

"Sometimes," I said, showing her through the door, "when we have company."

"Who sits there?" she asked hopefully, pointing to the small oval table in the window.

"Well sometimes we put the children there, if there isn't room at the big table for everybody."

Shirley Jayne was holding her ground firmly.

"Would you like to have your tea there with Elliot this afternoon?" I asked. She brightened up at that, looking to Elliot for approval.

"Sure!" said Elliot, shrugging his shoulders. So I reminded them that if they were going to sit in the dining room their manners had to be perfect, and with their vigorous nods of agreement we set a little table for two.

It was Christopher who was to become Elliot's best

friend at Carmyllie School. Christopher was four years older than Elliot, in Primary Six, but he was small for his age. Chris and Elliot struck up their friendship in the lunch room, making funny faces at each other across the room. Chris would pull his mouth apart with his two fingers, then Elliot would answer him by shooting a pea across the table with his spoon, or sticking a piece of macaroni in his nose. Chris dubbed him Elliot Macoroni. Then they would both get the giggles until Mrs. Brown, who was supposed to be keeping order in the lunchroom, banished one of them—usually Chris because he was bigger and supposed to know better—to the office door.

Chris, like Elliot, was something of a loner. He lived with his parents and two sisters in one of the council houses in the village, a tightly packed little row of gray-white stucco semidetached cottages behind the dairy farm. "We keep to ourselves, never mind the neighbors," explained Chris's father, Peter, a small man with a puckish grin who lived for motorcycles and Indian takeout. Unemployable for various obscure health complications that baffled the medical world, Peter spent his days in solitary consultation with the telly in a carpeted living room. Chris's mother, Lorie, who was also unemployable for medical reasons, studied feng shui and kept the house spotlessly clean. In spite of the narrow scope of Chris's life so far, he had an active imagination and a surprisingly open mind. He was not the least bit intimidated by the Guynd. He didn't believe in ghosts. He brightened up at the size of the rooms. "I love big houses!" he told me with confidence.

Chris was also capable of being very polite to grown-ups, which he'd long ago figured out was a super way to get into all kinds of mischief behind their backs. It was also a good way of getting fed between meals. Even knowing this, it was hard to resist Chris's apparently innocent charm, not to mention his genuine affection for Elliot.

Together Chris and Elliot roamed the fields and the woods, played hide-and-seek in the barley when it was up to their chins, jumped off the round hay bales. They climbed trees and made dams in the stream with sticks and stones. They fished for tadpoles in the derelict swimming pool. They fitted out buckets with rocks, pond greenery, and snails and watched the tadpoles over the course of a few days turn magically into frogs or, more often, toads. Then John would have to insist that they take the frogs down to what was left of the lake and say good-bye.

Chris's father Peter was fond of telling me that he had once worked as a gamekeeper, and whether or not this was true he was eager to impart to me and the boys his own brand of wisdom in that department. The habits and movements of animals—how to recognize the difference between deer and sheep tracks, how you can tell if a deer has rubbed its antlers against a tree—were of particular interest to Elliot and Chris. They would return to the house with high tales of their adventures. "We saw a fox!" or "Three deer crossed right in front of us in the den!"

Peter also helped to instill in the boys a certain contempt for others in the business, such as Brunton's gamekeeper, Mr. Shaw, whom they regularly encountered on his rounds through the Guynd in his Land Rover. One time Shaw brusquely told the boys that if they didn't move their bicycles off the road he'd run over them; it then became a challenge to see if they could get Mr. Shaw into trouble by annoying him. Another time they came upon him feeding the pheasants in the pen and took the keys from the seat of his Land Rover. They were planning to lock him into the pheasant pen but lost their courage when he spied them in the act. Still, it was exciting to report, "We saw Mr. Shaw! He was really rude to us!"

LIKE MANY RURAL communities in Scotland, Carmyllie is known as a parish, not a village. It's name in Celtic means "on top of a rocky or bare place," where once a castle stood. After the Reformation, the community that populated approximately twelve square miles surrounding this rocky, bare place gathered around the Presbyterian kirk where the castle was no more. The construction of the kirk, around 1609, was funded by the laird of the Guynd, at the time a fellow named Strachen. According to a statistical account of the area, it was in paying for the building of the kirk that Strachen went bankrupt and was forced to sell the Guynd to the Ouchterlonys. But such was the duty of the heritor under the stern eyes of the Scottish Presbytery. No one of any wealth would have dared to shirk his duty to the kirk any more than anyone would have dared not to make the trudge, however long, however foul the weather, to the kirk to spend the better part of a Sunday. During the service, elders scoured the villages for stragglers and idlers, rooting them out of their homes or reporting them to the kirk session.

Some 350 years later John's father donated a piece of the Guynd farmland near the kirk and paid for the construction of Carmyllie Hall for community events. This A-frame building was erected during an unfortunate slackening of architectural guidelines in the 1960s.

While Carmyllie Hall sticks out of the hillside like a visitation from another planet, the four-hundred-year-old kirk, with its lichen-covered stone walls, nearly merges with the landscape. Approaching it from down the road across the wide-open vista of farmland, it comes into focus like a ghostly apparition, framed by a dense grove of green-black trees. Having studied this apparition from a distance for some years, it seemed to me high time we found out if anyone ever went there.

One Sunday morning Elliot and I ventured inside, where an elderly usher beamed at us and enthusiastically motioned us in with a wave of his hand. The strains of a hard-pumping organ led a few pale voices in the opening hymn. About ten or twelve churchgoers, mostly over the age of sixty, were dotted among the otherwise empty pews, and a row of little heads could be seen in the front pew—the Sunday school. Elliot and I took our seats toward the back and were instantly offered a prayer book from our nearest neighbor.

It turned out to be communion Sunday. After the sermon the usher came around with a little tray full of glasses of red liquid. Pointing, he whispered hoarsely, "Ribena for the little ones!" Elliot's eyes lit up. Having downed the sticky sweek black currant drink, he was even more delighted with the folding tray at the back of each pew with holes just the right size to rest his glass in. Altogether Elliot decided that the kirk was quite cozy. And as we filed out the door our friendly minister shook my hand vigorously and expressed his hope that we would come again. Then he was off to his next parish in nearby Arbirlot, to preach to another six or seven of the village faithful there.

IN SCOTLAND THE SUMMER holidays are nearly as brief as summer itself—in olden times a ten-day stretch in mid-July, now closer to six weeks between early July and mid-August—which means that little effort is made toward children's summer programs. Some children are regularly shipped off to "Gran" for the better part of the holidays, many families disappear for a week or two south, and otherwise the summer plays itself out in old-fashioned formlessness.

There were always the various Scottish events to attend. We went to the Highland games at Cortachy castle (*Cor*-ta-kee) in the Glens. In a muddy field below the castle, burly Scotsmen in kilts competed in tests of strength such as "throwing the hammer," which involves swinging a twenty-pound weight on a stick around their heads, and then flinging it as far as possible. Legend has it that this tradition began five hundred years ago with village youths hurling the blacksmith's sledgehammer. "Tossing the caber" is another such game, in which contestants heave twenty-foot tree trunks from one end, aiming to land them upright at the other. Young girls in plaid skirts compete in the traditional "sword dance," hopping neatly between the crossed swords on a wooden stage. On the fringes of this spectacle, which nobody is following very closely other than the contestants themselves and their families, is a muddy fun fair of rides, spun sugar, local crafts for sale, and prize vegetables.

It seemed that most of these traditional events were nearly lost in the fringe activities that surrounded them, as a television program is lost in commercials. At the annual Games Fair at Scone (Scoon) Palace, for instance, the sheep dog demonstrations are hardly competition for the temporary shopping mall that is the main attraction, with its merchants' stalls selling fishing gear, smoked meats, Barbour jackets, guns, tartan blankets, and picnic gear. And virtually no outdoor event is worthy of its name without a "bouncy castle" on the side.

Weather permitting, there was always the beach at Lunan Bay. On one of those rare summer days when the sky was pure blue (well, almost pure blue) and the wind piped down to a gentle breeze, and the radio announced cheerily, "a very pleasant day over most of Britain," instead of the usual mind-bending confusion that passes for the weather forecast, I would say to Elliot, "it's a beach day!" We'd pack towels, a friend, a dog, and drive ten miles up the coast to a spectacular stretch of sandy beach and slide down the dunes.

Even on a good day, Lunan Bay was never crowded,

only bright with figures here and there in semi-undress, lolling in the sand, strolling, digging, the young and brave wading into the North Sea up to their waists, some in wet-suits actually swimming, romping dogs of every size and shape, and occasionally a horse and rider galloping by. On a bad day, there was always the indoor swimming pool at the high school in Arbroath. There I could sit reading in a plastic chair sipping a pale, vending-machine cappuccino, stripped down to a T-shirt in the humid, chlorinated air. Elliot and Chris cavorted in the pool with other small Arbroathians for an hour or so, finally emerging with red eyes and crinkly fingers.

There was the occasional invitation to go fishing. Martin, a childhood friend of John's, owned the fishing rights to a stretch of the North Esk River and charged customers for the use of it by the day and by the rod. For Martin and his wife, Monica, fishing was a job. They had to catch so many per season in order to "keep the count up," and thus to prove to their paying customers from Russia or the United States how lively a stretch of the North Esk they managed. This involved not only dedicated fishing on their part but also the regular use of a construction vehicle moving mud and rocks around to create a swifter flow of water or a deeper pool. Almost whenever or wherever we saw Martin and Monica they were dressed as if just up from the river, or just about to go down, probably both, weatherproof jackets thrown over layers of moth-eaten tweed and cashmere, and waders up to their knees.

Monica packed a gourmet picnic, and after throwing mash and withered lettuce at her population of 350 or so ducks that padded around the grounds of their concrete castle, we stumbled down the ravine to the riverbank on a gray day. "Gray days are best," Monica assured us. "You can see the fish better, and they're more subdued." She patiently taught Elliot how to cast and reel, cast and reel. Gray as it was we didn't see much or catch anything. "Actually the best time to fish is really about two in the morning," explained Monica, which is when she and Martin normally went out. Anyway, as we ate and drank from their generous picnic basket, sitting on a blanket on the stony riverbank, we digressed from the mechanics to the politics of fishing. Martin, who had an inexhaustble knowledge of the British class system, explained exactly how fishing fit into the mix.

"The tidal stretch of the river belongs to the crown, it's part of the queen's regalia," he explained, brushing the crumbs from his beard, "but the salmon fishing rights farther inland are the regalia minora, or lesser royal rights, so they're more or less up for grabs for anyone who wants to buy them, if you see what I mean." I had always thought that regalia had something to do with a parade, but if anyone could be counted on to prove my ignorance, it was Martin.

M and M, as we sometimes called them for short, also ran a commercial salmon fishing enterprise, a stretch of North Sea coastline for which they owned the netting rights. Every day when the tide was right for it their fishing crew took a boat out to haul in the catch. "Would Elliot like to go out with the fishermen one day?" Monica offered. Elliot was keen, but he wouldn't go without me. The day we chose turned out to be a stormy one. We approached "the Bodin," M and M's fishing cabin, along a narrow dirt road that curved along the edge of the seaside cliffs. Arriving at what felt like the coastline's outermost projection, we looked down at a defunct limekiln, a sea of whitecaps, and at our appointed launch, a big, leaky-looking, wooden rowboat shored up on a pebbly beach.

"Never ya mind the wind," said Joe, one of the three fishermen. "If ya fall overboard we'll catch ye," and he laughed a terrible toothless laugh and they all joined in, like something out of Robert Louis Stevenson's *Kidnapped*. But there was no turning back. Joe waded into the sea and held the boat steady for us. I picked up Elliot and popped him into the boat, and then Joe picked me up, and we were off, like it or not. It was a rocky ride. Water leaked through the cracks of our little vessel as we plunged along through the waves. Stopping and rocking at each buoy, Joe thrust his long stick into the sand to anchor the boat while the other two hauled in the nets, untangled a dead cormorant and threw it away, and gave the fish a whack on its head, though it continued to flip about around the floor of the boat. Elliot cringed at the sight and kept his fingers crossed on both hands until we returned safely to shore.

Elliot's social life not only broadened my own social scope, it forced me to learn my way around the county. I began to know people John did not know. I traveled roads and shortcuts he'd never taken. On those increasingly rare occasions when we drove somewhere together I heard myself saying things like, "If you take this right turn through Leysmill we'll come out just across from the road to Inverkeilor," as if I was the one who'd grown up here.

"Really? I would've . . ."

I knew gossip. I knew that other little boys and girls could be badly behaved behind their "pleases" and "thank yous." I'd had a glimpse of the darker shades of people's marriages, which John, over the banter of the dinner table or birthday party, couldn't see.

ELLIOT'S BIRTHDAY, falling on the ninth of July, inspired an evolving variety of traditions. It happened to fall at the peak of berry season, so we always went to one of those pick-your-own farms nearby, consuming as much on the spot as we brought back in our baskets. I made a sponge layer cake and Elliot studded it with strawberry halves laid into a bed of whipped cream.

Over the years we orchestrated all kinds of party games and attractions. One year a tug-of-war on the lawn, another, a chaotic and noisy game of capture the flag. Another time John sent a rocket into the sky that shot off a parachute, which was then supposed to take an aerial photograph of the Guynd, though I think we lost the film. There was a kite-flying birthday party, inspired by my childhood memories of an annual Fourth of July kite-flying contest in Ipswich, Massachusetts. Like the sea breezes of Ipswich, the wind at the Guynd was a pretty safe bet. Once, we got a kite as high as a small aircraft, or so it seemed.

Elliot's cousin James, a budding inventor at twenty-five, entertained the children with his self-designed, ultra-fuel-efficient "PPV," or pedal-petrol vehicle. This was a sort of tricycle for grown-ups, low to the ground, shaped like a bullet, and painted silver; with a bit of pedaling thrown in it gets 1,015 miles to the gallon. James was planning to pedal across Canada. To the children he was a superhero—incredibly fit, darkly handsome, and dressed from head to foot in black leather. They called him James Bond and some of the bolder boys were allowed to take a quick spin in the silver bullet.

We never failed to have some kind of treasure hunt, usually for candy, hidden in the bushes and the trees. This was inevitably carried out at top speed and was over in a trice, followed by a gathering of the treasure hunters under the oak tree, where they chortled and chewed, compared and traded their loot. One year after the party was over, Elliot and Gwen gathered up all the balloons from wherever the breezes had blown them—into the branches of trees, or across the wheat field, or stuck in the hedges. It was a treasure hunt all over again, until they were finally called inside for tea.

TEN

Tenants and Factors

...

ONCE UPON A TIME COUNTRY SOCIETY REVOLVED around places like the Guynd, with each estate conducting its own little orbit. It was like a village, in which all inhabitants played their role and knew their place. At the Guynd in the old days the *greive* (overseer) lived in the *parc neuk* (meaning the corner of the park near the farm buildings, now referred to as the farmhouse), estate workers lived in the cottages, unmarried farm hands in the *bothy,* and a gatekeeper at the lodge. The laird counted on this resident population to see that the estate ran smoothly—to tend the fields of the home farm, mind the chickens, fix the fences, clear the paths, and mend the roads. The laird was respected whether or not he was liked, for he offered a structure that gave shape and meaning to their lives and most of all security; he protected them from the unknowns of the world outside.

This feudal system persisted on the assumption that the land ultimately belonged to the crown and that the laird was a subvassal of the nobility, a leader in his community with responsibilities toward his subjects. They valued his opinion and his example, for he was one of them, in spite of his privilege, for his children went to school with their children, he withstood the lashings of a cruel winter as steadfastly as they did, he was their fellow Scot and thus no stranger to hardship. They counted on him to shelter them as long as they lived.

Nowadays the laird is apt to be looked upon not so much as a leader but as an outsider. His position is marginal; the government has taken over what was once his responsibility, that is, to shelter the people of the countryside. Machinery has taken over his role of employing people on the land. And his cottages have become part of the open rental market.

The cottages at the Guynd are still inhabited, not by farmworkers but by an erratic population of fugitives from the poorer quarters of Dundee and Arbroath. Art students, unmarried couples, the unemployed, the retired. Occasionally they might spend a day lifting tatties for a local farmer or banging in fence posts for John, if he pays them under the table so as not to compromise their unemployment status with the Department of Social Services. Being mainly the descendants of that class of feudal society who worked for the laird and in turn were looked after, they continue to expect to be looked after to this day. These are largely peaceful people, content as the cows in their fields, it seemed, as long as they have their telly and their cakes and tea.

"They call it the nanny state," said Martin. "As long as the government treats these people like children, they'll never really feel responsible for anything."

The laird is traditionally backed up by the factor, an office invented especially for the landed gentry; he is the middle man in the hierarchy of the rural classes. His job is to manage the rents, balance the books, and keep the laird abreast of the latest threats to his welfare, the latest wrinkle in tenants rights, the latest trends in farming practices. Condescending to those under him, obsequious to those above him, the factor easily makes himself unpopular with one or the other if not both. He's fair game. In the days of the Highland Clearances, when the big landowners cleared the clansmen off the land to make room for the more profitable population of sheep, it was the factor who did the nasty work, burning their sod houses to the ground, sometimes with people still inside them, too old or infirm to move. It was another Scot, Adam Smith, who indirectly caused the Clearances by advocating a profit-making society in the first place.

Today the factor is a slightly different animal. He works in an office, the same as that of an estate agent, and makes more money by selling property than by managing it, and furthermore there is always the hope that the new landowner will be easier to manage than the old. Meanwhile it is still the factor whose job it is to find the tenant, raise the rent, enforce the conditions of the let, and sometimes evict him, which doesn't make for a popular man.

But at least they know who he is. It's a good deal less clear with the laird. He goes to town—worldly, faraway towns like London. He travels abroad. He takes an American wife. They think he's rich because he owns the Guynd. Yet this worldly man is always dressed in work-clothes, and tattered ones at that. They see him splitting logs around the back of the house, or with his scythe, rhythmically swiping away at the tall grass along the drive, or raking over a mole heap, cursing under his breath, or out in his workshop, his fingers black with engine oil, trying to seduce a spare part of a lawn mower into the missing piece of a washing machine.

Once a fortnight or so the factor drives over in his Mercedes to have a quick look round. Though the factor never failed to put up a facade of friendliness and goodwill on his rounds, John hardly bothered to look up from his work. How could he trust a man who worked in an office, as if running a country estate were just a matter of shuffling numbers around on a page? He wasn't living it day to day. He didn't even deal with the tenants anymore, neither bringing them in nor, if necessary, getting them out.

There was a certain pattern to the comings and goings of these tenants that became apparent to me. To begin with they were usually desperate to move out of some densely populated housing estate in Dundee. Just looking for the peace and quiet that they imagined country life to be. But then, for one reason or another, they never seemed to stay very long. They arrived full of optimism, with buckets of paint and rolls of frilly curtains. They wanted a patch of garden, they promised to keep the yard tidy, they knew how to manage a coal stove. *Nae bother.* Was it the unstable nature of their lives, or the little disputes that arose with their neighbors, or simply that, having given it a go, they had to admit they would rather be in a warm, cramped council flat in Dundee? We were never entirely sure. They had their complaints. There was a leak in the roof, the chimney was blocked, there was a branch in the way of their television antenna. The laird could be slow to attend to these problems. He kept his own deadlines, not theirs. And then suddenly one day they were moving out, back to Dundee, or to some other town.

John regularly salvaged the things they left behind. "You wouldn't believe what they put in the bin!" A sound system. A file cabinet. A frying pan. Scattered outside the cottage were their larger castoffs. A refrigerator. A beat-up caravan. "This is worth money! All it needs is a clean!" But they did not aspire to John's thrifty ways. These were people on the move. As far as they were concerned, John's behavior was the quaint luxury of a man of property. So what if we reused the plastic yogurt containers, or if we salvaged the vegetable water for stock, while they drove five miles to Arbroath for Indian takeout. So what if we drove small, secondhand cars and endlessly repaired the twenty-year-old lawn mower. How could they feel any connection to this thrift when at the same time they couldn't help but notice that we were busy maintaining our social status, polishing the silver and brass, while delivery men unloaded cases of wine at our front door? How could they relate to the laird's fanatical exactitude on some matters when he was so lax about others?

Our constant hope was to attract tenants who struck that perfect balance, people who were both poor enough to seek cheap accommodations but enterprising enough to do a lot for themselves, people who were tidy, handy, self-sufficient, who knew how to raise animals and vegetables, who could tell the difference between a compost heap and a leaf mold, people, in short, who understood the old-fashioned ways of the country.

For a while, John believed he might have a handy person in Rory, who drove up to the front door one day in a rusty white pickup. Stepping out of the car, he was small and fair, slightly bow-legged. A gaunt black-haired woman looked out at us sideways from the passenger seat, as if she couldn't be seen. Like someone out of Walker Evans's Deep South, she was probably at least ten years younger than she looked. "Me and Claire here are looking for a place to live," said Rory. "Wondered if you had any cottages to let."

Claire lit a cigarette. "Me mum lives in Arbroath, she's not too well, see," she said, in a voice as deep as if it had been dredged from the bottom of the North Sea. "So I'm wantin' to be near her."

At the time there was nothing available. All three of the farm cottages were taken by art students from Dundee. A friend of Patrick's was in the lodge. He was supposed to be participating in a logging scheme but it appeared that he spent his days sleeping and his nights drinking beer in front of the telly, while his father, who owned a fruit business and drove a Jaguar, was covering the rent.

The only other building was the old farmhouse, the *parc neuk*, which was empty for the first time in thirty-odd years and needed a lot of work. It was only after old Mr. Fisher died the year before that we discovered the living room floor had caved in, the entire building was infested with damp, there was something amiss with the drains. Old Mr. Fisher had lived there since the sixties, paying a rent of five quid a week. The garden was littered up with a succession of dead cars, and the grass grew rank and wild. Occasionally his stooped little figure would emerge from the house and he would creep to the end of the drive, nodding at the tenants in the cottages, and then creep back again. But no one dared knock on his door, not even the factor, whose job it was, and Fisher never complained for fear that someone might disturb the squalor he called home. When he died he was given a pauper's funeral, and then the environmental health department pulled in with its skip to clear out the house.

Rory and Claire were not put off by the farmhouse. It was love at first sight. They were determined to move in, caved-in floor or not. It turned out that Claire had a green thumb and before long she had transformed Fisher's wilderness into a flower garden, rescuing old poppies and peonies and roses long since buried and tangled in neglect. She pruned the black currant bushes way back so that they could produce more fruit. She also had a way with dogs, so when we went off for the day or the night or the week, she was happy to take Foxy and Sugar. We talked about dogs and flowers. "Wantin' any cuttins?" she would ask me, and I always answered no thanks, until I eventually understood she meant flower cuttings, not curtains. But I wasn't as clever with flower cuttings as Claire. I admired her garden, asked her how she kept the bugs off the roses, how she moved the peonies. It was nice to get her to crack a smile once in a while. I thought about asking her if she wanted a job cleaning the house, but decided it wasn't worth the risk of ruining our relationship. She was so delicate.

Meanwhile, Rory was interested in taking up tree work, maybe hitch onto Patrick's wagon. Do some work around the Guynd. Elsewhere too. John was all for this plan and even put up the five hundred quid needed for the chain-saw course he was going to have to take to be legal.

For a while there was enough to pin our hopes on. Rory and Claire were runaways. We didn't know what misfortune or misadventure had driven them out of Dundee and we didn't care. As long as we had our understanding, that was all that mattered. Patrick too was willing to work with Rory, to educate him into the tree business. There was the memorable evening when John, Patrick, and Rory went out to celebrate their purchase of a secondhand portable sawmill. After a few pints at the Fisherman's Tavern in Dundee, Patrick took them on a road tour of all the dead elms he knew in Angus on which they were sure to make a killing.

Rory was also something of a mechanic. When John slipped on some wet leaves rounding the corner in

Monikie and put a dent in the back of the Escort, Rory did the body work. In exchange for work like this John gave him the old Land Rover to fix up and sell. Our business relationships were like that, quid pro quo, ad hoc, pro tem. We just felt our way. It was the way of the country, based on a certain kind of trust. Pretty soon Rory was the guy who had the keys to the big house, to get in when we were away, if he needed to. Sometimes I wondered, "Do we really trust Rory?"

"You have to trust someone," John answered, and that was as much as he could say.

He never touched the stuff, Rory said, when we presented him with a bottle of whisky at Christmastime. But I wondered why he always seemed to sleep so late, and why Claire showed up at our door in the middle of the night one time, asking if she could stay. Rory was in one of his moods, she said.

He went on two or three jaunts with Patrick, and cut a few limbs off some trees at the Guynd. After about two years, though, it was clear that he was neither energetic nor careful. His mechanic jobs were, as John put it, half-baked. John asked him to fix the log splitter but he couldn't figure it out; he was supposed to fix the cement mixer but having fiddled with its insides for a while took a much greater interest in painting the whole thing bright orange.

"It's an old military trick," said John. "Just paint it, and it looks fixed." Finally, after a row with John, Rory and Claire packed off, tired and bitter as we were.

Good tenants, useful or not, are hard to find.

The unpopular factor had suggested once that we put some capital into upgrading the farm cottages. The plumbing, the kitchen equipment, the heating all needed improvement. Clearly with a better class of building we would attract a better class of tenant, a more stable population, not to mention an increased income. It all made perfect sense to me.

"What do you think?" I asked John after the factor drove away.

"Where is this capital supposed to come from?" John returned, and before I could answer he provided his own with unmistakable contempt, "Stripping our assets, I suppose."

I suspected it wasn't just that upgrading the cottages involved a serious investment of time and money. John was not motivated to attract middle-class tenants to his property, with their middle-class expectations. He took no interest in obliging them. The last thing he said he wanted to be responsible for was the spread of suburbia. He despised everything that would follow in its wake—supermarkets, chain stores, fast food, waste. But there was another level to his resistance that he was probably not even conscious of. The last thing John wanted was to be surrounded by a community prosperous enough to undermine his position as their superior, a position he held, even in his rags and patches, over the financially vulnerable population attracted to the Guynd in its present state.

"What about holiday lets?" I asked John. "You can charge a lot of money for a short stay in the right season."

"I can just see you rushing around changing the sheets every fortnight," he answered. It wasn't changing the sheets that was going to be the problem. According to the stack of free literature I sent for, detailing the Scottish Tourist Board's guidelines for self-catering accommodations, the sheets would have to be fireproof, the upholstery cigarette and match resistant, the cookware unblemished, and the entire premises routinely tested and graded for safety, sanitation, maintenance, and so on.

"Anyway there's a demand for the cottages just as they are," John said, putting an end to the discussion.

John was right, I had to admit it. There was a market for inexpensive, namely substandard, housing in the countryside. Without even bothering to advertise, word of mouth attracted prospective tenants to our door on a regular basis.

"It's just that it's a crap shoot," I reminded John, "and so far we haven't been terribly lucky."

Along came Rachel, for instance, in her tight black jeans, leather jacket, chunky heels, and a gold stud in her nose. A single mother with an eleven-year-old girl, four horses, and two dogs, looking for a place to live. We could understand her wish to move out of Dundee and to live in the country.

"You don't look horsy," was the first thing I said to her. Yet if she was a little tough looking, we took her to be someone who was country-wise.

Rachel could have come "all Wellied up," she said, but wasn't sure which kind of impression she should try to make. An appealing candor, a way with words. Further-more, a woman with a child, a woman who cared for animals, was bound to behave in a responsible way, to be stable, to settle in for a while. A woman who could tell what kind of meal we fed our dogs with one glance at their stools was a woman who knew dogs. Her stock shot up. We showed her the fully furnished East flat in the basement of the house. The very next day she called to say that she really liked the place and that she was ready to run over with her deposit in cash. Why not, we figured. No other prospects had appeared. We invited her in for a cup of tea, showed her the terms of the lease, discussed the arrangements for the animals, and took her money.

Two weeks later Rachel moved in, directing the horse van through the front gate right past the CARS ONLY sign. Once the horses were out we could see that they weren't in great shape. One had badly cracked hooves, unshod. Another had a nasty scar across its face, as if someone had purposely hurt it. Soon one of our farm tenants was complaining that the horses were leaning over the fence and eating his kale. Meanwhile eleven-year-old Katie had set up a horse jump on the front lawn. John sharply reprimanded her. Once the holidays were over Katie didn't seem to be going to school. The shutters didn't open until past noon every day. "I think this woman is a disaster," John began to mutter.

Disaster eventually turned on the point that Rachel had brought a third dog, a male Staffordshire bull terrier, when we had specifically agreed to two aging cross-bred bitches, who we supposed would get along fine with our two. Rachel hung an old tire from the chestnut tree near Elliot's swing and goaded the dog into attacking it. I was beginning to doubt the wisdom of risking a bull terrier living anywhere near Elliot. Why hadn't she mentioned this dog, anyway? She was just taking care of it for a friend, she said, for a month or two.

"Then you'll have to put it in a kennel," I said. "There's a good one just up the road. Our dogs have been there. It's fine."

"That's not an option," Rachel replied in a new tone of voice. "If the dog goes, we all go."

"Fine," I said, tensing, amazed at my luck. By this time it was clear that we'd be better off with no tenant than with this one.

"She's blown it," said John, just as glad that it was me who had done the deed. I felt no compunction about demanding our rights as landlords against a tenant who had broken the terms of the lease, but for John it was more complicated. While he disdained the factor, that did not mean he was willing to do the factor's job.

I composed an eviction notice, polite but firm, suggesting that while we understood that Rachel would need some time to find a new place to live, we hoped that her move would go as swiftly and smoothly as possible.

What had begun as a regular country arrangement between landlord and tenant was about to turn into a class conflict. With heroic Scottish figures like Rob Roy in her mythical past, Rachel may have felt justified in holding her ground against the heartless landowner. The unknowns of everyone's past rushed forward in blind combat. The full spigot of lowlife Dundee now opened wide. Rachel threatened to take her time moving out. "We'll be movin', " she promised, spitting every word out with demonic satisfaction, "but it may not be as 'swift and smooth' as you would like. We think it's lovely here," she taunted.

The next Saturday a huge horse van pulled up. I breathed a sigh of relief as they loaded up. Next, Rachel roared up to the front door in a white hatchback. She stepped out of the driver's seat; a couple of cowering young men peered out the windows as she strutted up to the front door in her black leather jacket and high-heeled boots. "What are your plans, Rachel?" I asked.

Her plans were to get her deposit back, as well as the cost of removing her horses. "We can't give you your deposit back until you've moved out," I said, trying to make this sound like a normal transaction, trying to remember the rules while confronting a woman who was clearly in the habit of writing her own. She threatened to stay put until she had her money. "I'll have to discuss it with John," I said, hedging.

Back underground, apparently packing up her things, Rachel kept up a steady barrage of phone calls. "If I don't have my money back before tomorrow," she threatened, "the charade will go on."

Upstairs I twitched and worried, certain that her threatening tone was not altogether empty. "Maybe we should give her back her deposit tonight?" I suggested to

John. No, he insisted. We didn't even know if she'd paid the rent, and couldn't find out until Monday. Finally, sometime after dark, Rachel knocked at the front door for the last time. It echoed through the darkened hall. John opened an upstairs window and leaned out.

"Give me back my deposit!" Rachel cried, standing outside her loaded van with the motor running.

"Tomorrow! Business hours!" answered John, and shut the window.

"Then we'll be stayin,' " we heard her shout.

The next morning all was quiet. The van was gone. And no, we learned she hadn't paid the rent. But it was over. For a few hours we lived in tentative peace. It wasn't until late in the afternoon that we discovered she had stripped the place. We called the police.

It's a little easier to catch a thief when you know who she is. With an unusually quick response from the Tayside Police we recovered most of the furniture two days later. Rachel had apparently driven her borrowed van full of our furniture along the antiques trail, unloading a bit here, a bit there, and blithely leaving her name with the dealers. Just a few hours later, Constable Ogilvie and John were on the same route, recovering a bit here, a bit there.

"You know," said Constable Ogilvie when he came to make his report after the burglary, "you have to wonder why a person would want to live way out here in the middle of nowhere."

At least the charade was over. At least we thought it was. I couldn't help wondering if it might go on, as Rachel had promised it would. She had been identified by the police, but she was still at large. Late one afternoon Stephen thought he recognized her white hatchback driving away from the house. It sped away as soon as he spotted it.

One night in early November, when John was away in London, I was awakened by the sharp barking of Foxy and Sugar, both of them suddenly howling at once, up and running down the stairs. I lay in bed, frozen. Then I heard the sharp bark of a smaller dog in the distance. Somebody was prowling around outside. I groped for the clock. It was one o'clock in the morning.

The whole house was dark as pitch. I got out of bed, praying that Elliot would not wake up, flicked on the light at the stairs, and crept down to the front hall where the dogs were baying. I let them out the front door into the darkness and listened for the sharp bark of the small dog, but it was suddenly quiet. Had I imagined it? I went back inside, into the kitchen, turned on the fluorescent light, and decided to leave it humming all night. But back in bed I lay stiff for a long time, listening.

About three weeks later we had a Christmas crafts party for Elliot and a few other children and their mothers. We set up in the dining room with scissors and paste, origami paper and stencils, popcorn and cranberries, gold paint and pinecones and walnuts. For two hours that afternoon and into the evening, mothers and children peacefully crafted and chatted and ate shortbread and drank tea. By the end of it I was too tired to tidy up and left everything where it was.

It was one of those still nights, warm for December, hardly a breeze. We went to bed. In the middle of the night I shook myself awake from a bad dream. There was a children's party, and there was an intruder, and I was just getting ready to confront him when I woke up in a panic. Thank God, I thought, it was only a dream. I got up and went to the bathroom, flushed the toilet, and went back to bed.

In the morning when I went downstairs, I noticed that the front door wasn't quite closed. That was odd. Then I went into the dining room where the remains of the crafts party were still scattered about. But what was the Delftware plate doing off the wall and lying on one of the chairs? The children hadn't done that, had they? Then I noticed that the door of the sideboard was hanging open. And a drawer was missing, the one with the spoons. The silver candlesticks were gone. I started moving around the house, quickening my pace, heart pounding, mouth dry. In the library the ottoman was open and the blanket was missing from inside. The pair of Chinese jars were gone from the mantel piece. In the drawing room the china cabinet was open. Stripped bare except for a few chipped pieces. I climbed the stairs to waken John. "We've been robbed again," I said.

Why hadn't the dogs barked? Because they were shut up in the kitchen to keep warm and didn't even hear the burglars? Or had they been seduced with a piece of steak? We looked at Sugar. She looked back, thumped her tail on the floor. How much more would the thieves have taken if my dream hadn't wakened me in the middle of their work and my movements hadn't frightened them away? Why wasn't the front door locked? Why didn't we have an alarm?

"We've got to get better security, John." I tried my weary voice, later that day. "How many times do we have to be hit before you see that?"

No answer.

"I'm going to call that alarm company in Dundee and set up an appointment. Tomorrow."

"We can devise our own alarm system. It would be a lot cheaper," said John, calmly.

"Who cares about cheap when we're being robbed left and right?" Now I'm hysterical. "We need a system that works! We need *something* that works!"

The next day I phoned three alarm companies in Dundee and set up separate appointments for them to come out. I chose the Electroguard people, because they seemed the most familiar with the area. They installed a keypad near the front door and assigned us our secret code. Little red lights set in the high corners of the rooms blinked on and off as we passed under them. They tacked up a large white plastic control box over the front door which read ELECTROGUARD in bright red letters. Ugly as it was, it made me feel better.

"Do we have to have that sign there?" asked John irritably. "Now they'll know we have an alarm."

"That's the whole point," I said. "That's ninety-nine percent of it." I think John was more interested in catching the thieves than in warding them off.

I had always assumed that the country was a safer place than the city, and that country people were more honest, and more neighborly, than city people. I thought that being remote equaled being safe, that it was crowds and anonymity that allowed for criminals. But now I was learning that the country had its own dangers, its own variety of thieves. They weren't after your wallet or your videocamera, they didn't rob banks or siphon off corporate funds. They were poachers after wildlife, roof tiles, garden ornaments. I was learning that the combination of a prominent house, obviously stuffed with antiques, and a remote house, half a mile in from the main road, was as promising a prospect as a thief could dream of. We weren't the only victims. Country houses all over Britain were regularly burgled of everything from the family silver to the iron boot scrape on the front doorstep.

Further down the hierarchy, the petty thieves came after raw building materials, which with any luck we would never notice were gone. But John knew where everything was, and precisely how much there was of it. "Somebody's been nicking the roof tiles down at the farm!" he would say one day, or on another, "There's been a poacher in the woods, you can tell, empty cartridges bloody everywhere."

Having the house alarmed wasn't going to keep the poachers away. Another layer of security was needed to seal off the estate. Martin and Monica had four German shepherds, a continuously running videocamera, and high iron gates at the drive, which they controlled remotely from either the castle or the car. We started to keep the front gate closed, chained and padlocked, opening it only for special guests. But the farm entrance had no gate. I spent several hours on the phone one day to automatic gate companies all over Britain. And another few more hours sizing up the farm entrance, exactly how far in the gate should be, what height, how wide, and considering questions like operating it with a key or keypad, or card. What about the postie? The skip men? The farmers? Was the confusion this would cause worth the small degree of security it would provide?

We were rich in property but poor in our ability to maintain it. A place with an air of dereliction about it was all the more attractive to thieves, as it looked like an easy target, as easy as an old gentleman with a cane and a frayed collar is to a pickpocket. "If we can't afford to maintain it, we can't afford it, period," became my refrain. Was there any point in having so much, if safeguarding it was almost all we could think about? Were we to become players in that awful kind of tragic farce, prisoners of our own possessions? We were living in a place that was designed around the assumption of a cooperative working relationship between landlord and tenant, and which now seemed only to force an uncomfortable intimacy between them.

One day an odd-looking woman knocked on the front door. She had long dark hair, a kerchief tight around her head, and layers of colorful clothing. She seemed to be alone and to have arrived on foot.

"Can I help you?" I asked her.

Instead of answering she took my hand and began to tell my fortune. "I see a young boy child," she said (though it didn't take a psychic to see that from the litter of toy vehicles on the doorstep). "Your husband works hard" (anyone would have to work hard on a place like this). "You are far from your home" (she had detected a foreign accent), you miss your family, but you will return."

Then she produced a white crocheted pillowcase and told me that it was mine for only twenty-five pounds. Might the Gypsy's crocheted pillowcase buy us some good luck? If nothing else I hoped it would keep the other members of her tribe at bay. I remembered the Gypsies in Sir Walter Scott's *Guy Mannering*, following their expulsion from the estate of Ellengowan. "Ride your ways, Laird of Ellengowan" cried the devilish Meg Merrilies as the Gypsy procession made their way. "This day ye have quenched seven smoking hearths—see if the fire in your ain parlour burn the blyther for that."

I took her crocheted pillowcase, bought her off for twenty-five quid, and waved her away down the road.

ELEVEN

Guests and Ghosts

. . .

THERE STILL REMAINED THE GNARLY QUESTION OF
the old house by the garden, the original Guynd house,
where the first three generations of Ouchterlonys at the
Guynd had lived and died. A quarter of a mile from the
mansion house, it was completely concealed by trees. It
didn't stare back at us forlornly from across the South
Park, but we knew it was there. Every year or so John
would get up a ladder to repair a few slipping slates on the
roof and secure the piece of sheet metal over the big hole.
He had always dreamed of restoring it; the house held a
special place in John's heart. Indeed anyone with a heart
could see its charm—the sitting room with its rounded
bay window looking out over the *burn* to the fields
beyond, its two-story hall with a minstrels' gallery at one
end and Gothic-arched door leading to the garden at the
other, its hidden staircases and secret rooms. Even in its
present state, or perhaps because of its haunted, dilapidated beauty, the old house could easily set a healthy imagi-

nation on fire. John had started to restore it one summer some thirty years ago, as far as installing some plumbing and electricity. But there were rooms with missing floorboards, the windows needed reglazing, central heating, or some form of heating, had to be worked into the fabric of the building. It was a big job.

Every summer we lived in dread of vandals, like the two teenage boys who camped in the house and broke all the windows in a drunken fantasy of driving out "the gray lady." From then on the word had circulated among adventurous teenagers in Arbroath that there was a haunted house at the Guynd, and we were constantly on the alert. An unknown vehicle spied across the field on the back drive would set us running down there to check. Some of our intruders were cautious. Often we didn't notice them until they had come and gone, leaving their telltale cigarette butts and empty beer cans. Others were less so. They pretended not to notice that they were on private property. One summer evening a carload of teenagers drove right behind the big house, tires squealing. I ran out and yelled at them, "Hey, slow down! What do you think you're doing here?"

"We're lookin' for the haunted hoose!" they yelled exuberantly. Cheeky as can be. Drunk as skunks.

"Well there isn't any haunted house here," I told them, "so you better just drive on out the same way you came in. Don't you know this is private property!"

Another time Morag, who kept her horses at the farm, alerted us to a car she had seen parked near the old house.

I grabbed my Nikon and with John and Elliot ran down to the house just in time to spy the rascals—about six of them—through the open front door, climbing the stairs.

"Okay you guys," I called, "come out and get your pictures taken!" As the wayward youths trooped out, I snapped pictures of them, hangdog and embarrassed, stealing glances at me as they squeezed into their little Ford. I took a picture of that too. I was catching on now. A license plate number is always a handy piece of evidence to show the police.

"Interesting," said John after they were gone. "They won't argue with a woman, especially a woman with a camera and an American accent!"

Still, how were we ever to make headway with the old house, when it was so prone to vandalism? Where would we find the initiative, when there were so many other jobs to be done? It was clear that we were never going to get down to this project without an impetus from somewhere or someone outside of ourselves. I had tried the Landmark Trust, a nonprofit group that rescues charming, derelict, and superfluous buildings on old estates and transforms them into tasteful holiday lets, channeling the profits into their next effort. But the trust was so overwhelmed with offers they couldn't even find the time to come to see us. I had filled out an application to Historic Scotland for a grant to repair the roof, but only as far as the section where they ask you for the name of a qualified architect to oversee the project.

"What do they want an architect over here for?" cried

John. "It's a bloody roof job. How much is an architect going to cost?" And so on.

For some time we had been discussing the problem of the old house in a more or less serious way with Max, an old friend and colleague of mine, an American living in London. Max was divorced and freelance, struggling to make ends meet between magazine assignments in order to write his epic historical novel. All he needed was a place to live, rent free, for as long as it took him to write it. Max had already visited the Guynd on the occasional weekend. He had studied John at close range—in his element—and admired him for his ingenuity and his independence, and also, I suspected, as an authentic native curiosity who might add some colorful patches to one of his characters. John admired Max, too, for his lively mind, and his store of literary references, the depth of it far beyond John's own classical education. If John quoted a line from Milton, Max could quote the next line, and the one before it. They were as different as chalk and cheese, as Alison would say, but they found each other fascinating; they got along.

I can't remember now whether I said to Max, well there's always the old house, or if he said, might there be somewhere at the Guynd where I could live and be helpful, but we began to talk about his coming to live in Scotland as a real possibility. I don't think I really believed he would ever pack up and come, any more than I ever really believed we would get around to restoring the old house, but it was perhaps a good thing for him to feel that there were options out there, and for us too to talk about it, to toss it around. And then suddenly he was coming.

Max arrived at the Edinburgh airport in late July. I didn't recognize him at first, had to go around the loop twice before I spotted him. It was the Stetson hat that threw me. Was he trying to stand out like a palm tree on a prairie? Then the thought passed as he piled his three duffel bags into the boot of the car and his large frame into the passenger seat and we whizzed off, talking about his flight, the weather, the best route to the Forth Bridge. Then, as we cruised up the A92, he spoke of his visions of helping to restore the old house, of making it his home. He already had a plan, an elaborate schedule of priorities, in his mind.

We were blessed with plenty of sunshine that summer. Our target was to get the old house habitable—or at least parts of it—by the time the weather turned in the autumn. After a week Max moved out of the guest room and down to the East flat, which was empty, so that we could all have more privacy. If this was to be a long-term arrangement, it was important to establish his independence from the start. All we expected of him, we told Max, was to cover his own electricity and telephone bills.

There was a good table in the East flat, large and sturdy enough to work on, eat on, both. And a modern armchair and sofa, left by one of our tenants. Max and I found the various pieces of an old double bed in the laundry and put it together with a moderately clean box spring and mattress. He needed sheets, towels. We scoured the collection of extra kitchen utensils in the cellar, selecting various cooking pots and pans, flatware, colander, spatula. He needed a telephone—one of our old rotary phones would do for now—and he needed his own phone number. He wanted music. John set him up with an old stereo system and a big pair of speakers.

I would take Max into Arbroath to shop at the Safeway and then leave him to explore the town on his own. He would come back on the bus with a couple of secondhand sweaters and a half a dozen old jazz LPs from the charity shop. Thinking ahead to the winter, Max made plans to store up a supply of food in the freezer. From the Fisherman's Association he bought a big white plastic industrial apron, such as they wear at the fishmongers' for cleaning fish; from the neighboring farmer he bought a ten-pound bag of potatoes, a stash of onions and carrots, and started cooking up a winter's supply of soup. The whine of Duke Ellington's jazz music and Max humming along emanated from the East flat as the kitchen windows steamed up with the heat of his bubbling cauldron.

After all our trials with local tenants, with the natives of this land, with people who were supposed to know how to live in the country, we were willing to take a chance with someone like Max. If he didn't necessarily understand the ways of the culture he now found himself in, he was intelligent and resourceful. If he wasn't especially handy, that was all right too. We were more interested in someone who simply cared, someone who didn't have class issues with us, who had his own creative work to get on with. I was beginning to think that it was people like

Stephen and Max—artists and writers—who were our best neighbors in the long run. I had even fantasized about turning the whole place into an artists' colony, a sort of Scottish Yaddo, with each guest assigned to his or her own private studio and everyone gathering for dinner and lively discussions at the end of the day.

John too enjoyed the idea of being, by way of sheltering Max, a kind of patron of the arts. Furthermore, it was a familiar arrangement in the country—creative, penniless bachelors sheltered by their more settled married friends. Simon and Kate, for instance, had Alex, an old school chum, living free in a cottage in exchange for gardening work while he carved stone in his spare time. David and Tarka had Nick, a classmate of David's, living over the stables in exchange for tutoring the boys while he finished his screenplay. These interesting men were part of the scene, part of the family, while at the same time they remained refreshingly unattached. With the extra space that life in the country offered, it seemed, there was equally the need for the extra man. A woman in the country needed not just one man, perhaps, but two. Certainly I was ready for the company of a man who shared my interests in history and writing. I had at times felt keenly the shortage of such company, as if a piece of myself had been put away in a drawer. And as my fellow American, Max would be my ally; we would share an American perspective and wrestle with the problems of the culture gap together.

As usual John was distracted by a variety of unexpected chores—cows out, broken fence, new tenants in the lodge—and work on the old house was continually post-poned. To pass the time I took Max to the vegetable garden for a session of weeding. I showed him where to dump the compost, how to pull the stinging nettle, when the broad beans were ripe for picking, how to deadhead the flowers. Max went about these tasks somewhat distracted-ly, pausing in the midst of his work to quote Wordsworth, or Coleridge, or Pope.

"All things fall and are built again, and those that build them again are gay," he quoted Yeats. "That's us!" he cried.

I wondered if it would be great works of literature that would carry Max through the long Scottish winters; How much solitude he could take; how much physical discomfort he was fit for. Even in those balmy August days Max was lighting the coal stove in the East flat in the middle of the afternoon, while a modest log fire after dark was all I'd learned to expect. On the two-mile walk to the temple and back he frequently needed to stop and catch his breath. I tried to prepare him for the cold, the darkness of winter, the wet. "You won't want to be standing at the bus stop for half an hour on a November evening in the pouring rain," I warned him.

"I don't mind rain," he answered. "I won't melt!" And then he would recount in detail his camping adventures in Canada with his son, by way of explaining how capable he was at adapting to rough circumstances. Whatever, the gardening wasn't going to come naturally to him, I could tell, even less than it did for me. Max was much more interested in turning his hand to the restoration of the old house, which he was already beginning to furnish and decorate in his mind's eye.

I myself had often dreamed of fixing it up. I had dreamed of moving out of the mansion and into this smaller, older, and in many ways more charming house, someday. I had mulled over the colors of the walls, arranged the furniture, hung the pictures. I was throwing parties in the hall, complete with musicians in the minstrels' gallery, while our guests wandered through the Gothic arched door into the garden and back again. All it took, I believed, just like Max, was a vision.

"What can I do," Max asked John when the work was ready to begin. John suggested that he could start by clearing the weeds around the outside of the house.

"And after that," John added, "if you take a ladder down there, I'll show you where the gutters need clearing out."

Before the day was out Max had given up on the gutter job. "The ladder slipped. I got nervous. I have to confess I'm afraid of heights." But there was no shortage of other jobs to be done—stripping the walls and making them ready for paint, for instance. That should keep Max busy for a while. John fixed him up with a bucket, a sponge, and a scraper and sent him off again.

"I keep telling you," John said to me with a sigh, "it takes more time to set people up than to do the job yourself!"

Max hated to work alone. He easily persuaded Elliot

and Chris to get into the act. What child could resist the
miracle of bringing a haunted house back to life? For
years they had played and explored around the old house,
fighting their way through the jungle of Japanese
knotweed down below, building dams across the *burn*, tee-
tering on fallen trees, and prowling with the dogs up the
ravine on the other side, looking for foxes and deer. Max
adored the company of these young boys. He fed their
imaginations with stories and fantasies, and they, in turn,
were flattered by his attention, intrigued by his childlike
excitement and his deep, confidential voice, as if everything was a secret, just between them. They took old
swords from the basement and hacked away at the weeds
around the house, vanquishing the enemy. They joyfully
tore old wallpaper from the walls and ripped up rotting
linoleum from the kitchen floor, stuffing bags and bags
full of rubbish. "You missed a spot," Max would say,
pointing to a shred of wallpaper still clinging to the wall.

In the evening, as a reward for their labors, Max would
drive the boys into Arbroath for fish and chips. They
would sit on the stone wall in the harbor looking at the
fishing boats and teasing the seagulls with their leftovers.
Max read *Harry Potter and the Sorcerer's Stone* so that he
could discuss the book with them. Elliot would quiz him
(in which house is Nearly Headless Nick the resident
ghost?) to make sure he'd read it carefully. In the East flat,
Max reserved a cupboard for the boys to keep their secret
treasures in, padlocked it, and gave them the key.

I would come and go to the old house to check in on

Max's progress, to cheer him along, to see if he needed anything, and was usually seduced into conversation. There he'd be, up the ladder, ready to let forth whatever was on his mind, whether it was an underrated jazz singer like Anita O'Day, or a mutual friend in London, or a movie we had both loved or hated. We imagined how beautiful the house was going to be. "Look at the light in here," said Max. "It's at least two f-stops brighter than yesterday!"

We pondered the life of John's ancestors. Which rooms did they live in? What was the view from upstairs like when they lived here? How big were the trees? How high was the water? What grew in the garden?

Almost every day we touched on the irresistible topic of how the Scots use language, what the various local expressions meant, or how the meaning of a word might change from one language to the other. This was a favorite for both of us, fellow Americans, fellow writers. I told him everything I knew.

"Never say *pants*," I warned him, "unless you mean underpants. They're trousers, here." And never say *English* when you mean *Scottish;* they're not the same." Or I might explain, "To Americans, *proper* means British, or stuffy, or something they equate with Britishness. But in fact, proper here means *the right way to do things,* as in 'a proper cup of tea.' See?" I tutored him in the subtleties of pronunciation. "Here, it isn't *in*novative, it's in*nova*-tive, it isn't *mi*scellany, it's misc*ell*any, it isn't a dynasty, it's a dinnasty."

And of course we talked about writing. My biography of Walker Evans was complete and published and it was time to embark on a new project. But I was so far from my sources in Scotland, so out of touch with my field and my colleagues. "Use that as an advantage," Max advised. "Try another kind of writing, something more personal. I know you've got it in you. You should write a novel. You should write about this place."

We talked about how to get started. How to do research. How useful or not was the Internet. How to be honest and true. "Just write what you feel, Belinda," Max would say slowly, like a mantra, closing his eyes, "just write what you feel, and it will ring true."

"What about *your* writing?" I asked Max. "Have you started?"

"No, not yet, I'm reading," he answered. "I need to get more settled before I can write."

HAVING BOUGHT a secondhand car for six hundred quid, Max set about exploring the countryside and the little towns of Angus, enchanted by all he saw. He observed the world in broad strokes and big references. The landscape was a Claude Lorrain. The village was out of Dickens. The child was a Bellini. "I went to Brechin," he announced at the end of one such day. "I loved it. I could live the rest of my life in Brechin." The more dull and plodding and gray the town, the more he was entranced with it. I must have been missing something. He discovered secondhand bookshops I never even knew were there. He frequented car boot sales and antiques shops and the Salvation Army store. He'd be gone most of the afternoon, bringing back potato mashers, saltcellars, napkin rings, and teacups. I thought we had offered him all that stuff from the cellar. Why was he spending his money on it? It was the thrill of the hunt. He would twirl the thing in his hand as if it were gold. "Look! Look what I found today!" he said, holding up a quaint little toast rack. "I learned a new use of the word brilliant. They say that here when they've taken your money."

"Either that or *smashing*, I answered, "or sometimes *luvly*. I gave it my best Scottish lilt. "Or *grrrand*."

"The people here are so friendly," said Max.

"Do you think so?" I wondered. I used to think so too. But now I suspected that they engaged you in conversation only to confirm that you were a foreigner. They were sizing you up. Are you here on holiday? I was frequently asked, which I usually took to mean, is she going to need help counting her change? But there was no need to spoil it for Max. "They're supposed to be even friendlier in the Highlands."

At the end of every day Max would appear on the front doorstep. He needed something. He had a question. We'd invite him in for tea, to share the newspaper, to talk. "I'm a naive here," he would begin with great deference, warming up to his question. From me he asked for guidance in the way of manners and society, from John the best way to do the job. In spite of his impatience to get it done, Max seemed ready to learn from the master. "I'm beginning to understand your husband," Max told me one day. "I know that everything he does, even if it looks careless, is done for a reason. For instance, the watering cans are left upside down in the sink. Why? Ah! Because they are made of metal, and will rust if they are not properly drained."

Yet in doing it—scraping the walls of layers of paint and old wallpaper with the tools John had given him to use—Max couldn't resist trying to improve on John's method. Anxious to see results, he bought a little electric sander and went to great lengths to demonstrate its greater efficiency to John. He made two samples, side by side on the wall, and timed his work, proving that the sander was faster. John remained unimpressed with Max's detailed diagrams and continued to advocate the old sponge-and-scraper method. It was cleaner, less mess to clean up. Max hadn't factored in the cleanup time.

"Fools rush in," sighed John, to quote a favorite saying.

I COULDN'T HELP wondering if John wasn't also jealous of the progress Max and I were making, envious of our finding pleasure in the changes, and humor in the obstacles. The pleasure made him itchy. The humor seemed to be at his expense. We were foreigners, naifs, clueless Americans, getting off on each other's fantasies. But how could we squander Max's enthusiasm, I wanted to know. How could John be fussy about method when, after all, the job was getting done?

As much as he was enjoying getting to know the culture and seeing the old house come to life, Max was increasingly agitated about his lack of control over the work schedule. He wanted to work as if he was going to a job, he wanted deadlines. He wrote long lists of the jobs that needed to get done before he could move in, outlining the things he could do alone and the things he needed John's help with. It was all terribly logical.

I tried to break it to Max—I thought he knew—that things would happen as each priority made itself most urgently felt, or when the opportunity arose. It was hard to explain. John simply hated anyone getting ahead of him. Nothing annoyed him more than a car speeding past him on the road, except perhaps a car that was hanging on his tail. "But I promise you, Max," I assured him, "John will get the job done when he really has to. Like the dining room. It had to be done in time for the charity luncheon. And guess what! It was."

Then I argued Max's point privately to John. "Look," said John, "you know perfectly well we don't work like that here. Anyway, he's perfectly comfortable. He's living rent free. Why doesn't he just get on with his writing?"

But with every passing day Max's needs, Max's questions, seemed to multiply, as quickly as John's excuses to put them off. It was beginning to seem that they were trying to outwit each other, each marshaling their own esoteric brand of knowledge and expression—John with his engineering know-how and gut-level sense of how things work; Max with his intellectual logic and facile verbal manipulations and references—diabolically demanding of the other what they knew was impossible. It became a subtle tournament of annoyance, with me as ineffectual middleman. Now Max wanted to discuss with John the details of his bookshelves—how the books would be arranged alphabetically, regardless of size, but how, on the other hand, he would need his reference books at waist level so they were within easy reach. There was the bigger question. Should the bookshelves be properly built into the house, out of serious wood, or should we just erect makeshift prefab shelving, in the interest of time. John was for making them properly; Max was more interested in speed.

There were the books he was shipping up from London, he explained in elaborate detail one evening by the fire, and then there were the books he was collecting every other day or so from secondhand bookshops. "A complete set of the Waverley novels by Sir Walter Scott!" he would declare triumphantly upon his return. *"The Pleasure of Ruins,* by Rose Macaulay. And look, *August Follies,* by Angela Thirkell, and *Pomfret Towers!* She's a great unsung writer, you must read these, Belinda. I got them for you."

Max felt obliged to educate me in the connections between what he had been reading in English literature for years and what was now spread out for him in real life, as if he were the first to discover it. But no matter how much Max had read of Scott or Thirkell, it could not be held as superior to my nine years of real-life experience. As much as I enjoyed explaining the culture to Max, it was draining, and I resented the very idea that I should be obliged to bottle it up for him, and hand it over, in exchange for his recommended reading.

"And these are for Elliot, *The Once and Future King*, by T. H. White, he'll be ready for these soon."

Max delivered this speech from his usual seat of command, the largest armchair by the fire, which I had had resprung and reupholstered some years back. Not that it was my personal chair, it wasn't anybody's chair. But I couldn't help thinking it presumptuous the way Max never failed to claim it. When he came up for a drink in the evening, no other chair would do. He would land in it heavily, settling contentedly, even if my glass or book was beside it, and I had risen only to let him in the door. Oh that's my glass and book, I would say, taking them away. But it never registered. Or if it did, he chose to ignore it.

"You really like that chair," I finally said one evening.

"I love this chair," he confessed. "I want this chair."

The chair became an issue. "I have to have a comfortable chair," Max told me very firmly one day. "I read five hours a day. I need a chair to read in." The armchair in the East flat wasn't going to do. I could see that. I took him down to the farm buildings to inspect an old sofa suite that was in pretty good shape. He could have any or all of it. He tried sitting in one chair, bounced a bit, wasn't sure. Like Papa Bear. This one's too small, that one's too big, that one's too soft, this one's too hard. Well, maybe it would do, he'd think about it.

When was he going to start writing, I wondered. He'd been with us for more than a month.

Then came the day when John was under the floorboards of the old house fishing an electric wire through to Kenny, who we'd hired to help, in the next room. I arrived with Elliot and a bunch of tools. Max was looking agitated. There he was, up the ladder with his scraper while the two engineers actually seemed to be enjoying the intricate job of feeding wires to each other. There was a dialogue between them that Max could not penetrate. "Why don't we just lay them down on the floor with duct tape?" Max wanted to know. "it would be a lot faster."

"Not at two hundred and fifty volts!" said John.

Kenny chuckled.

As soon as he saw me, Max started talking again about his need for a chair. "I must have that chair today!"

"Can we talk about this a little bit later? There are a few things going on at once here," I said. I looked at John, on his back, fishing the wire under the floorboards, while Max, grandly covered in plaster dust, stood on his ladder.

Later, Max turned up at the front door, with the refrain, "I must have that chair!"

"You'll just have to wait until John gets down to the farm with the wagon," I said. "It could be two or three days." Then I had another thought, "Either that or you can make your own arrangements to move the stuff."

"Who's going to pay?" asked Max, planting his feet firmly on the ground, standing very straight, looking at me very hard, gray as a November fog.

Who's going to pay?

Had I ever expected so much from John, so fast, even at my most starry-eyed?

"Maybe *you* will," I heard myself saying out loud. For a change, I said to myself.

Max retreated to his basement flat and became very quiet for about three days. There were no questions. There were no requests. His car would go out, and come back. If I passed him on my way around the back and said "Hi, Max!" he would just nod. Finally, with a note, he summoned me downstairs.

"Max wants to talk to me," I told John, after Elliot had gone to bed. "I suppose I should try to sort this out."

As soon as I entered the flat Max started his tirade. He began tense and quiet. John was incapable of organizing anything, he could work only for himself, and by himself, he was mean, he had no remorse. It got worse. He traded on his class! He didn't deserve the Guynd! And finally, "I'm not his slave!"

"He's not your slave either!" I shouted, standing up.

Max ordered me to sit down and listen. I was actually too mesmerized to do anything else. I was glued to my chair. I was learning something new about the workings of Max's mind. I was testing my own strength against his blast.

He went on. "This place is a shit hole. This chair is a piece of shit. This colander—look at it—it has no legs. I don't want your castoffs! You have to live with him, but I don't!"

As I listened I groped for the balance between Max's truth and mine, between my loyalty to Max—my friend, my fellow American—and my loyalty to John. Scotland had imposed a new kind of structure on our relationship. I was the lady of the manor and Max was our penurious intellectual guest, a type who turns up in English novels to provide another point of view, to add an ironic bite or twist to the values or aspirations of the society. Max and I had been colleagues and equals on the neutral turf of the city, but now we were mistress and pet. Neither of us knew how that one went.

There was no way I could walk the thin line between my loyalties. Max was insisting that I choose, and condemning what he already knew would be my choice. For if he was to be the loser he was going to be sure to leave destruction in his wake, to leave the indelible imprint of his having been there and passed judgment. There we sat, at the bottom of the house, while he ranted with a will to shake its very foundations, as if to bring the whole pile down on top of us.

Yet the edifice stood firm. John had hardly swayed under the heavy winds of the American idealist. He knew his obligations to the house and to the land, and because of this he possessed an unassailable power over the rest of us. I had been around long enough to know. It didn't matter much to John whether Max stayed or went, any more than anyone else. People come and go, the winds blow this way and that. He'd seen too many failures in his time to honor Max's as anything spectacular. How much did it really matter that he could recite forty stanzas of *Paradise Lost?* That he'd read *Tristram Shandy* and *Martin Chuzzlewit?* John was the edifice, even if the rest of us were human. And the knowledge of this made me calm. I listened quietly.

Everyone comes to the Guynd with his or her own fantasy of what should happen, until he realizes that it won't.

I finally rose from my chair at three a.m., leaving Max to his chair, the despised chair.

"You're a dreamer, Max," I said in departing. "I understand. I'm a dreamer too."

JOHN LAY AWAKE in the darkness of our bedroom at three in the morning.

"Goodness, that was a long talk."

"Well, you know Max," I said. I lay there, trying to find the balance. Who was the man lying next to me? And who was the man downstairs? Which one was crazier than the other?

A few days later, without a word, Max quietly packed up and slipped away, leaving nothing behind but a vat of frozen potato soup, a complete set of the Waverley novels, and a 350-pound phone bill.

TWELVE

The Birthday

...

IN 1999, THE LAST YEAR OF THE CENTURY, WE COULD legitimately claim that the Guynd mansion house was two hundred years old. The architect's drawings were dated 1799, dodging the eclectic building boom of the nineteenth century by a hair. However long it took to build the Guynd house—perhaps fifteen years—1799 was the only date that was clearly documented, the date of its conception.

"Maybe we should give the house a birthday party," I suggested to John. He resolutely ignored his own birthdays. I think he believed that if he ignored them they wouldn't count. And to some extent this strategy seemed to work for him. He sailed into his sixties without a gray hair on his head or an ounce of fat around his midriff. When our eyes met, really met, his could still penetrate, beaming steadily out of their deep hollows. His hands were strong, articulate, working hands, and the skin of his cheek was as soft as a baby's, even if lined with the inimitable signature of passing years, like a tree. "There's no need to celebrate, as far as I'm concerned," John would say about his birthday, and then quickly change the subject. But a birthday party for the house was another matter altogether.

"What a good idea!" he said immediately. In fact, one of the very few good ideas I'd had lately.

While John had battled change every step of the way, he would by now have to admit that the house could boast many improvements. I could hardly count them all. By this time John would not even bother to notice if I moved a chair or rehung a picture. He could manage a tentative smile at Mr. Sturrock, the upholsterer, when he rolled up in his van to carry off another armchair to his shop. "Is that all of them now?" John would ask hopefully.

"Not quite," I'd reply, catching Mr. Sturrock's eye. He was accustomed to the wary reception of his clients' husbands.

All the rooms had undergone a gradual transformation, as I groped my way over the years toward a coherent decorating plan. There was still that worrisome crack in the library ceiling, the cupola leaked in a heavy rain, the drawing room needed repainting, the window sashes needed work, and one of the shades in the drawing room absolutely refused to reach the top. But I no longer stood squinting incessantly at the rooms, trying to figure out what was missing, what was jarring, planning my next angle of attack. I didn't hungrily scan decorating books and other people's houses for ideas. My heart no longer

raced at the sight of a toile de Jouy cotton print or braid-
ed silk trim, and I didn't lust after sisal/wool floor covering or lose sleep over pencil pleats. My efforts to strip
down were finally relaxing into filling up again. My lists
of things to do were shortening, finally disbanding into
sporadic notes. And I had given up arguing with John
about the kitchen. It was what it was. It was his.

The hall was bright yellow, spacious, and welcoming,
with its marbled columns and flagstone floor, like a warm,
sheltered courtyard; the niches in the corners with their
vases of boxwood and the round table center stage with its
piles of mail and bowl of keys; the jumble of gardening
tools and walking sticks and Wellington boots by the door.
Nothing was pretending to be out of sight under the staircase, nothing but a wicker dog basket.

The dining room was grand and stately, in red, white,
and Deep Worcester Blue. Over the sideboard the tar-
patched Virgin with grapes, after Mignard had long since
been replaced with exotic birds, after Snyders. The floor
was still scored by the movement of the Wrens' cots in
wartime, but how could that bother me when all the chairs
matched and only one had been chewed by a dog? How
many dinner parties we had hosted around that table, from
my first shy attempt with a thin beef stew for six to a fairly confident roast turkey for twelve? "I can't believe how
calm you are," Alison would say, as a dinner party
approached, but that would be because she had taken care
of the puddings. How I had enjoyed selecting the right silverware from the sideboard, placing them just so, choos-

ing the glasses from the cupboard, place mats from the drawer—generations of wedding gifts still giving pleasure. And would I ever get over the charm of looking into this commodious room to the barnyard sound of bleating sheep in the background, that such elegance belonged to a farmhouse? And then the faces lit up by wine and candlelight, the movement of new courses, the shifting topics of conversation, the interruptions of excited children, the bursts of laughter and quiet murmurs of confidentiality amidst the din. John Ouchterlony, Esq., silently smiling in the glow of his picture light, presided over the scene where in his day the gents would have paused after dinner with their port and Stilton while the ladies withdrew to the drawing room.

By day the library was a thoroughfare. By night it was the end of the road, with its richly textured greens and reds waiting to receive us by the fire. The same old books on the shelves—referenced on the odd occasion—the same rotting, bedraggled leather fringe. On the tables the stacks of books and half-read magazines, folded over mid-article—*The New Yorker* (mine), *Private Eye* (John's), and *Country Life* (ours). With its motifs of tangled leaves and wild animals, the library was dark and deep, like a woodland.

Through the arched doorway the drawing room opened up like a sunny garden with its off-whites and light, neutral pinks, its floral chintz cushions tossed around the various chairs, its gilt-edged mirrors reflecting the outside in. The room held its various attractions at any time of day—a jigsaw puzzle might be in the works, chess set ready, and Elliot's toy pirate ship bearing down across a sea of blue carpet toward a small farm behind a chair— but especially at teatime when the afternoon light beckoned us down to the bowed end of the room, overlooking the lawn. With children and dogs, books and newspapers, and whatever the business of the day, we came to sit, to talk, to read, to doze. With the house full of family or houseguests we rallied in the drawing room for a game of charades. Or toward the end of an especially jovial dinner party, someone might be persuaded to play the piano, and a few dinner guests well fortified with wine gathered around and burst into ragged song, while others stretched their legs in front of the fire in the library and continued their conversations unabated.

These were the moments in which I basked briefly in an overall sense of success in achieving the kind of life I believed the house was made for. If the family ghosts were watching, surely they would have smiled.

To celebrate the Guynd, 1799–1999, we invited about sixty people from all over the county and beyond to come for drinks. "I wish you could be here," I wrote to my parents, who had by now given up transatlantic travel, "we've made so many improvements to the house since you were last here." They would simply have to imagine how years of their example in the art of entertaining was finally playing out in their youngest daughter, three thousand miles away in a country house in northeast Scotland.

As the guests arrived and filled the space, the ground

floor, with its high ceilings and wide doorways and its long stretch of reception rooms, easily distributed and absorbed the crowd. From anywhere I stood I could take in the whole scene. "The house was *made* for parties," said Rosalinde, decisively.

"New cushions?" asked Tess, inspecting the drawing room. "I always like to see what you've done."

"You've really made the place feel like a home," said Rita. "I never really liked this house before."

"Ah, the Guynd hasn't changed a bit," said Alistair, an old friend of the family who hadn't been there for some thirty years. Was this supposed to be a compliment or a little put-down to the American upstart, veiled as a compliment? Was Alistair simply blind? Or was the imposing architecture of the house all that mattered anyway? Never mind my injections of color, my rearrangements of furniture, pictures, and objects, my tortured decisions over the years.

"Actually, it's completely changed," I told Alistair, as politely as I could, having decided that he was blind. "It's just that you can't see it."

On the other hand, to take Alistair's word as a compliment, I had to admit that I could hardly "see it" myself. I had achieved what had once seemed to me the impossible. I had brought in the new without startling the old. They lived comfortably, seamlessly together in what was now our house, our layers of living years together. It was becoming increasingly difficult for me to recall exactly how these rooms looked and felt when I first entered them nine years earlier, so slowly had they metamorphosed. Piece by piece. Like a homemade soup of stock and leftovers evolving over a period of days, becoming more rich and unexpectedly right by degrees. In fact—in a moment of daring—I even threw in Doreen's forty-year-old raspberry vinegar, and I think it made all the difference.

AS THE MILLENNIUM approached we contemplated another kind of celebration. We had traditionally spent Hogmanay with Rita and David at their farm in Perthshire, beginning with dinner for four or six of us, a roast leg of one of Rita's rare breeds of sheep along with plenty of red wine, affectionate ribbing and gossip, and carrying on with the traditional first footing around the village after midnight. But this year Rita and David were planning a bonfire on their hill and inviting all their neighbors.

"As much as I love Rita and David, does it really make sense to spend this Hogmanay on top of a hill with *their* neighbors?" I asked John. "Maybe we should be spending it with our own neighbors. Why not have a bonfire here?"

In the true spirit of Hogmanay, as Rita had taught me, I meant our closest neighbors, not those at the far corners of the county but our tenants and neighboring farmers, nobody farther away than Carmyllie. Finally, in those last days of that last year of the century, it seemed that we had something to celebrate. The Guynd was beginning to feel like the self-contained community that it was designed to be, and perhaps was, in the best of times, back in the days when John's grandparents hosted Sunday school picnics on the lawn by the lake and an annual luncheon for the tenantry; back in the days when I imagined laird and tenant bonded in mutual respect and shared objectives. Finally it seemed that we had the kinds of tenants we needed, enterprising old-timers, quite capable of taking care of themselves, accepting the limitations of the rustic life and equally gratified by its special pleasures.

An elderly couple, Anne and Will Tully, had settled into the lodge. "I've had my eye on this little cottage for years," said Willy. "Drove by here I don't know how many times." They did it up with lacy curtains and pile carpets and embossed floral wallpaper, hung pictures of stags and trout streams and decorated the mantelpiece with figurines. "That's how I like to see things," said Willy, "nice and tidy-like."

It looked as if the Tullys were going to be with us for the long stretch. Willy was a retired gamekeeper. They came with ferrets, which they kept in a cage by the stone wall, for catching rabbits, and a dozen or so hens. Undaunted by the task of doing up the lodge, they already had their eye on the farmhouse, which had been empty since Rory and Claire had moved out. They had also taken over the old U-shaped piggery to use as a henhouse and erected a fence across the courtyard, so that what had been overgrown with weeds was now pecked down to the ground. In exchange for the use of the piggery, fresh eggs were ours for the asking. "Needin' any eggs?" was the first question the Tullys asked whenever we met. The tower of egg boxes on the stairs went down, down, down until there was but one, which we traded back and forth; when it was empty they filled it up.

"I told you those egg boxes would be useful one day," said John.

"Looks like one is all we need," I replied.

Throughout the day the Tullys traveled regularly between the lodge at the front gate and the piggery at the farm, passing by the back of the house, and sometimes the front, on foot or by car. Never nosy, they just kept their eye on things.

By October Willy's sister Davina had moved into the North Cottage with their eighty-three-year-old mother, Violet. Anne's sister and brother-in-law, Sam, were planning to move into the lodge as soon as the Tullys moved into the farmhouse, and Sam's daughter and her husband were going to rent the bothy and come over from Glasgow on weekends. By summer the vegetable garden at the farm was all ordered rows of beetroot and cabbage and everything was to be shared.

"Them beets is coming up nice, eh," Will Tully would say. We took their beets, they took our potatoes. Typical Scots, they favored root vegetables and were suspicious of anything green. "How do you cook that spinach, Belinda?" Willy asked me, warily.

"Makes a great soup," I told him. "Or pasta sauce. Or just cook it plain!"

He noticed the sprigs of lovage, like some anonymous weed—though more carefully clutched—in my hand. "You eat that stuff?" he asked me skeptically.

"Sure, I tear it up and put it in the salad."

"You eat anything green, don't you," he said, shaking his head, giving up.

"Americans do," said Anne, sagely.

Stephen, who had been with us longer than any other tenant, took over Will Crighton's job, mowing the lawns, trimming the hedges, and cleaning up fallen trees and branches. Stephen cared about the landscape, and unlike John, Stephen didn't mind using a chain saw.

"He'll never cut anything down, not John," said Will Tully, looking at an overgrown, wind-beaten yew in front of the house. "It's just not in his nature, is it?"

"He'll be thinking about the mess it leaves behind," I agreed.

Tully knew there were some things you could change in a person, and some things you couldn't. He knew when to ask, and when not to ask, just do.

The millennium bonfire struck all of our tenants as a fine idea, and John, with their interest behind it, thought so too. The only question was where to celebrate. "Maybe if we started it in the old garden, all the trees would catch fire." I suggested to John, half joking. "At least that would be one way to clear it!"

"Maybe," said John. I wasn't sure if he was serious. "And we could use the old house for the party. Get a keg of some nice beer from the Fisherman's Tavern." Then I knew he was serious.

The keg of beer would be set up in the kitchen of the old house, so the kitchen had to be made warm, not so much for the sake of the company as for the sake of the beer. "Nothing worse than a cold beer on a cold night," says John. So he went about constructing a wood-burning stove out of an old tin barrel with a door at one end, for stoking, and a chimney liner at the other, and hooked it up.

At least three days before New Year's Eve, John and Stephen started moving fallen trees in the garden to clear a space for the bonfire. While Stephen got busy with a chain saw, Elliot and Chris delivered bag loads of sawdust and rubbish out of the workshop in a wheelbarrow. These would form the innermost inflammable core of the bonfire. John taught them how to build up the structure like a wigwam, and to stuff the sticks and branches into the weave so they stuck. For three days they worked until it was almost as tall as the old house and looked like a witch's lair.

New Year's Eve was a dead calm night. After a late dinner, about half an hour before midnight, we headed down to the garden. John had made candle lanterns from the sawed-off bottoms of plastic tonic bottles fitted with wire handles for the children, Elliot, Chris, and Stephen's daughter, Gwen. Stephen carried a torch and cousin James arrived with sparklers. We followed their trail of bobbing candlelight and crackling sparks down the road to the old house, where a steady stream of smoke had been curling out of the chimney for hours, warming the beer.

The Tullys were already there with a bottle of whisky, Davina and Violet were perched on some of our sturdier castoff chairs. The beer keg, with its shiny pump and spigot, was ready for action and John deemed it the perfect temperature. Chris's family came along—his parents, Peter and Laurie, and the girls, Katherine and Rachel. Sandy and Bev, the young couple who now lived in the north cottage, came up from the farm.

Gwen was keeping her eye on the time. "It's five minutes to midnight!" And so, beer glasses in hand, we all headed out to the garden and stood in the clearing around the wigwam, its branches reaching up crookedly against the moonlit sky. John lit a torch, as Gwen counted down, "Eight seconds to midnight, seven . . . six . . . five . . . four . . . three . . . two . . . one!" and John set fire to the innermost pyre. A flame shot up, sparks flying ahead of it and dancing into the sky, and the assembled fifteen or so faces glowed with warmth and firelight and the contentment of a job well done, a certain clearing of the air. Five miles away the sky over Arbroath lit up with a sudden glow and the distant crackling of millennial fireworks.

I AWOKE THE next morning with a heavy head, anything but ready to greet the millennium in daylight, wan as it was. I didn't have to get out of bed to know what the dining room would look like. The remains of merriment littering the dinner table—party poppers, empty wineglasses, sticky plates. I considered the fact that if I was quick, I could quietly snag the last helping of trifle for my breakfast. But then I would have to look at the kitchen. And I knew that if I donned jacket and gloves and headed down to the garden our glorious bonfire would be a little pile of smoldering ashes. The fire that the night before had been so mighty and bright would barely give off a breath of warmth, and all around it the old garden a chaos of fallen timber and overgrown Christmas trees.

What had once sharpened the senses now dulled them, like a song you've played too many times.

Marriage is like a house, I thought, staring up at a crack in the bedroom ceiling. It's a shelter, first of all. And it needs to be kept in good repair. Signs of water seeping through the wall need to be investigated before the paint begins to flake off, a bare patch is exposed, the fabric begins to crack, and the job of fixing it is too discouraging, too expensive, simply the last thing you can be bothered to do.

While the ghosts of John's parents and the pall of their bitter marriage had retreated under the layers of our own activities and routines, was it only by virtue of the fact that John and I were now filling their shoes, sliding into their roles as strangers to each other, or, just as often, enemies? Our little squabbles and resentments, built up into deep piles, unresolved and unresolvable, had gathered like so much junk in the basement. "Why can't we just clear it out?" I had cried. How many times.

"There's enough to do," was his reply to anything he didn't wish to do and never even intended to do. He did not wish to investigate the basement, to get to the bottom of it all. To John it was part of the structure of the house, it felt like home, and he dared not disturb it lest it fall down.

For John the duties of his legacy were bound to a house, and to a landscape. This was the material proof of his reason to be, the gift that he must give back to the world, that he must not squander, that he could not abandon.

Surprise visitors regularly reinforced John's sense of loyalty to the last vestiges of the family tree in Angus, the custodian of the holy grail. To me they reinforced something else: the encouraging fact that the name had seeded and flourished elsewhere in the world. Like the two blond girls in blue jeans who drove up in a Volvo one late summer day. One of them, speaking careful but perfect English, introduced herself as Karin Ouchterlony. She was from Sweden, she said. Her parents had encouraged her to seek out their family origins while she was touring Scotland. With the help of an ordnance survey map of the area, she and her friend had found their way to the Guynd. Perhaps, with any luck, some distant cousin would still be there to open the door. John appeared from around the back of the house. "We are somehow related," Karin explained, "though very distantly."

It was late afternoon. We invited them in for tea. They both said "Ahh," in just the right way as we showed them into the front hall. We led them through the library into the drawing room. We showed them the architect's drawings, the survey of the farmland, the portrait of John Ouchterlony, Esquire. After tea they asked if there was a place nearby where they could camp. We offered them the lawn, and then, on second thought, because they were so nice we offered them the spare room, and pretty soon I was hunting down one of those spare tins of tomatoes to cook up a spaghetti sauce for supper. They went out sight-seeing the next day—to Forfar and to the Glens—and then came back and spent another night.

Then there was a fellow named Lony who showed up one day from Tennessee; he was small with soft features and dark hair and he didn't look Scottish at all, yet he'd discovered that his name was originally *Ouchter*lony, about 250 years ago. He was in Scotland on business and taking some time out to do some genealogical research. A visit to the public library in Forfar eventually led him to our front door, the only house in Angus where an actual Ouchterlony might still be found on the ancestral turf. We showed him around the house, swapped family history anecdotes over a drink. "Seeing this means more to me than words can express," he wrote, upon parting, in the guest book. "Joseph (Ouchter)Lony."

The Canadian cousins came over occasionally, now three healthy and happy generations descended from John's uncle Guy Ouchterlony, the one who drowned in the lake. They came in parties of two or three, to check in on the old homestead, so grateful that we were keeping the place together so that they could make the occasional dive into family history, pore over the picture albums and the Colonel's diary, and walk to the temple.

IT WAS AFTER ONE such visit that I finally decided to attack the black box. It had been waiting for me in the wine cellar. It was about the size of a very large bread bin, only it was black instead of white and, instead of "Bread," written on it was "Mrs. Ouchterlony's Trust." I knew that it was full of accounts. There they were, all neatly bundled and tied with pink solicitor's ribbon and stuffed into the depths of the black metal box like so many bones. The folds of those 150-year-old documents resisted my prying fingers like a coffin. Might something in here shed some light on the mysterious John Ouchterlony, the poet of the temple, the man for whom the house was built? Might knowing him better help us to understand what we should be doing here and why?

In his will John Ouchterlony had spelled out every article of furniture, bedding, farm equipment, and live-stock, every piece of silverware and jewelry down to the silver buttons on his waistcoat, and thoughtfully matched them to a long list of family members and friends that he expected to survive him. He bequeathed his library to his aunt Ann Milne, his portfolio of forty color views of Switzerland to his friend George Douglas, his stock of wine and Madeira to the Whim Club in Edinburgh, and he requested that his body clothes be divided equally between his house servant and the gardener. The Guynd estate would pass to his two surviving sisters, Mrs. Cumming and Mrs. Pearson, and to his nephew, James Pearson. He also stated his wish that his servants and other inhabitants of the estate "should possess the houses and gardens presently possessed by them rent free during all the remainder of their lives." He asked for a simple funeral, "to be conducted with as little show or expense . . . without ostentation, as my life has been," and to be buried next to his grandmother in the church graveyard in Montrose. He thanked God for preserving him from having any enemies, and he trusted that he should die at peace with all men.

A six-page memorandum of John Ouchterlony's last days and final hours had been dutifully penned by his old friend Dr. Thomson, who for several months had been attending to his declining health. As the laird's symptoms worsened, he summoned the doctor to his bedside daily. He confided in the doctor that he knew people supposed he was on bad terms with his sisters and their families, but that in fact they were on the best of terms and he much regretted that he could not ask them to be with him during his last illness "for want of accommodations at the Guynd for ladies."

On the morning of November 29, 1843, the doctor found his patient much worse. His throat was badly swollen and he was nearly speechless with pain. Papers, letters, books, and clothing lay about all over the floor of his bedroom where the doctor held vigil and sought in every way possible to comfort him. In spite of the untidiness of his rooms his mind was highly organized. Every door and every drawer had a key all its own, and he knew exactly which key fitted which hole. He pointed to a slate and pencil and wrote, "I am dying," and then, with his slate and pencil, haltingly directed the doctor to this drawer or that cupboard for the papers, drawings, promissory notes, coins, silver, and jewelry he wished to distribute among his family and friends. Finally, he insisted that Dr. Thomson himself take a receipt for 298 pounds "for his kindness," and would not rest until the doctor had located it and laid it on his pillow and assured him that he understood. Just after three o'clock in the afternoon of that day, "Mr. Ouchterlony breathed his last without pain."

This scene, as I soon realized, took place in the old house by the garden. The morning after his death, wrote the doctor, the executors removed the papers and books and clothing that lay about and placed them in a press. Then they ceremoniously marched up to the "new" mansion house, which stood empty, where the decorative woodwork was unfinished and the drawing room floor had never been laid. In the library they found that the shelves were full of books and specimens of mineralogy and a few pebble buttons mounted in silver. The doors to the other rooms in the house were locked, and the keys could not be found. The executors then nailed up windows where they were insecure, and boarded them over where they were missing, and with the heavy iron key they locked the big front door.

So the rumors about the poet of the temple were right. He never did move into the mansion house that was built for him. He remained in the old house by the garden and left the mansion unfinished and unoccupied for fifty years. While he may have intended to move in some day, he regarded the entire enterprise not so much as a personal ambition as "a debt he ow'd." In his poem he laments, "how short his life who bade these forests live," but his faith in future generations of Ouchterlonys made his own "fleeting span" exempt from the pressure to change. Hanging on, holding his ground, was enough. From the accounts of later generations, his heirs inherited "a wilderness."

Darwin wrote, "It isn't the strongest of the species that survive, nor the most intelligent, but those most adaptable to change."

"You'll never change," I had said once to John in a moment of frustration.

"I don't have to change," he replied in all innocence. Which suddenly rendered all the changes I had struggled to make over the years entirely unnecessary and selfish and the plan I thought we had made together nothing more than the material of an ongoing discussion, like an empty mansion house with a few books on the library shelves, waiting for us to move in.

"Do you assume that Elliot will want to take over the Guynd when he grows up?" I would ask John from time to time. Here was our boy, raised on muddy roads and tractors, on wild blackberries and big country dogs, at home with silver spoons and grape scissors, ancestral portraits and tasseled keys. He understood instinctively the ways of the country. He had a taste for both the rugged and the genteel, the rough and the smooth, the intricate and the plain. He was at home in a cottage or in a castle. It was a balance that was such a rare and irreplaceable privilege. The Guynd was his cradle, his castle, his island.

"Well it's a piece of the landscape, isn't it," was John's usual answer. "It's not everybody who has that. And you'll never have it again," he warned. Did never having it again mean that you had to have it?

John's contemporaries by now had sons that were grown men, already taking over some of the responsibilities of the estate, already residing in some smaller house on the property, preparing to take over, as their fathers entered their sixties. There was a fifty-five-year age gap between John and Elliot, however. How were we to fill this gap? What would happen between John being too old to manage the Guynd, and Elliot being too young?

IN THE MORNING quiet of the first day of the new year, the new millennium, I bundled up in layers of fleece and crept into my study. At my desk, I opened a drawer and dived once more into the unfiltered past. In one, a collection of dried-up thirty-year-old shoe polish. In another, a string collection I didn't even know about, and a bag of small change from Iceland. An envelope bulging with fragments of gilded picture frames, which John's mother had carefully put away for mending, if only we knew which fragment belonged to which frame. A heavy bundle of iron keys we would never match to the various drawers and cupboards and doors they once sealed. A bill from P. Shearer and Son for eight yards of Orkney tweed for two pounds and twelve shillings, dated the eighteenth of August, 1936. Stamped paid. How much more meaningful shopping was in those days! A transaction like buying a bolt of tweed was an event worth commemorating. But now, what to do with this extraordinary piece of printed ephemera, with its five different ornate Victorian typefaces and flourishing signatures? Frame it? Throw it out? Put it back. Close the drawer.

Opening another, I found a blue envelope, addressed to Doreen from her cousin Peter Percival, canceled stamp, 1966. "I wonder if perhaps the time has not come for a new approach," he wrote. "You have tried for years to compete with conditions as they turned up. I doubt whether anyone but you would have stood it so long."

Outside the window clouds were moving west, or was it north. In New York my apartment had a northern exposure; the clouds moved in only one direction—to the right. Here they move every which way. The day had started out in tentative sunshine, but now a dark cloud hovered ominously. There seemed to be a patch of rain over Arbroath. The sea was obscured in fog where just this morning it had sparkled. But I was used to the skies of this fickle maritime climate. If it starts out gray, it will turn blue. If it starts out blue, it will turn gray. O clouds, unfold!

"It is no longer a question of patching up and making do," wrote Peter Percival to Doreen.

Why did I marry him? It was one of those moments in life when the forces of attraction drew us into a bond, and we decided to trust those forces as our guide. A more skeptical pair might have predicted the unlikelihood of the match. But John and I shared a belief in the unlikely, even though, as I was eventually to understand, that belief came from different sources. Put to the reality test over a period of ten years, it's something else. Mine from curiosity and optimism—a sense of adventure and of new worlds to conquer; John's from despair—of time running out, of his last chance to save the Guynd. And for some time it felt like the same thing.

Why did I marry him? He asked me to. It's not every man that does that. No, come to think of it, he never actually asked me to. "It's all yours if you want it," he said.

"I said that?" he asked me, incredulous, years later. He was really offering himself, but he thought of himself as the house. No, he was really offering his house but as he was one of the things in the house—part of the baggage that comes with it—he was offering himself. Having married them—the man and his house—I discovered that they belonged first to each other, and only after that to anyone else. They had a grip on each other greater than mine on either of them. This fortress of a house and of a man had defeated me. It was one thing to vanquish the ghosts as they had once dominated the physical space around us, but another to banish their trace in our minds. I knew when I married the man I had married the mansion. Now I knew that neither the house nor the man—no matter how much I may have influenced them for a time—would ever be truly mine.

Acknowledgments

. . .

I wish to thank my many patient readers over the years, especially those who offered constructive criticism: Rita Adam, Lucinda Baxter, Carol Bundy, Wendy MacNeil, Victoria Munroe, Elliot Ouchterlony, John Ouchterlony, Rosamond Purcell, Barbara Pinkerton, Katya Slive, Julia Thacker, Marty Townsend, Joe Umphres, Ike Williams, my editor Jim Mairs, my agent, Charles Everitt, and my copy editor, Donald Kennison.

Sources

LOCAL HISTORY, COUNTY OF ANGUS

Allan, J. R. *The Northeast Lowlands of Scotland.* London: R. Hale, 1952.

Forfarshire Illustrated. Dundee: Gershom Cumming, 1848.

Fraser, Duncan. *The Smugglers.* Montrose: Standard Press, 1971.

Illsey, W. A., ed. *The County of Angus, The Third Statistical Account of Scotland.* Arbroath: The Herald Press, 1977.

Jervise, Andrew. *Land of the Lindsays.* Edinburgh: Sutherland & Knox, 1853.

————. *Memorials of Angus and the Mearns.* Edinburgh: Adam and Charles Black, 1861.

John Ouchterlony of Guynd, *Account of the Shire of Forfar,* 1682.

M'bain, J. M. *Eminent Arbroathians.* Arbroath: Brodie and Salmond, 1897.

Warden, Alexander J. *A History of Angus and Forfarshire* (in five volumes). Dundee: Charles Alexander & Co., 1880.

SOCIAL HISTORY, SCOTLAND

Cannadine, David. *The Decline and Fall of the British Aristocracy.* New Haven: Yale University Press, 1990.

————. *The Pleasures of the Past.* New York and London: W. W. Norton & Co., 1991.

Graham, Henry Grey. *The Social Life of Scotland in the Eighteenth Century* (in two volumes). London: Adam and Charles Black, 1899.

Herman, Arthur. *How the Scots Invented the Modern World.* New York: Crown Publishers, 2001.

Johnson, Samuel and James Boswell. *Journey to the Hebrides*. Edinburgh: Canongate Classics, 1996.

Linklater, Magnus and Robin Denniston, eds. *Anatomy of Scotland*. Edinburgh: Chambers, Ltd., 1992.

McEwan, John. *Who Owns Scotland*. Edinburgh: Polygon Books, 1977, 1981.

Smout, T. C. *History of the Scottish People, 1560–1830*. Glasgow: William Collins, 1969.

Wightman, Andy. *Who Owns Scotland*. Edinburgh: Canongate, 1996.

ARCHITECTURE AND LANDSCAPE DESIGN

Brewer, John. *The Pleasures of the Imagination*. London: HarperCollins, 1997.

Campbell, Susan. *Walled Kitchen Gardens*. Shire Publications, 1998.

Girouard, Mark. *Life in the English Country House*. New Haven: Yale University Press, 1978.

Loudon, *Mrs. Loudon's Lady's Country Companion*. Longman, Brown, Green & Longman's, 1845.

Morley, John. *Regency Design, 1790–1840*. New York: Harry N. Abrams, Inc., 1993.

Robinson, William. *The Wild Garden*. New York: Scribner & Welford, 1881.

Taitt, A. A. *The Landscape Garden in Scotland*. Edinburgh: Edinburgh University Press, 1980.

THE COUNTRY HOUSE IN THE TWENTIETH CENTURY

Robinson, John Martin. *The Country House at War*. London: Bodley Head, 1989.

Seebohm, Caroline. *The Country House: A Wartime History*. London: Weidenfeld and Nicolson, 1989.

Strong, Roy; Marcus Binney, and John Harris. *The Destruction of the Country House*. London: Thames & Hudson, 1974.

ARCHIVES

Arbroath Library
Guynd archives and family papers, at Guynd
Scottish Register's Office, Edinburgh

ABOUT THE AUTHOR

BELINDA RATHBONE is a photography historian who has written widely on modern and contemporary photographers. She has contributed essays to numerous books and is the author of *Walker Evans: A Biography*, a *New York Times* Notable Book of 1995. She lives with her son, Elliot, in Cambridge, Massachusetts.